Jack's Country
by Paul Peacock

A new edition of the book originally entitled
Jack Hargreaves - A Portrait
with the addition of
an Appendix by kind permission of Simon Baddeley
'How *Out of Town* and *Old Country* were produced' by Dave Knowles
and new photographs that bring Jack's television story up to date.

Cover illustration by
John Ryder, graphic artist for *Out of Town*, Southern Television

Jack's Country
by Paul Peacock

All rights reserved. No part of the publication may be reproduced or transmitted by any means or in any form without prior permission by Little Knoll Press

The copyright for this book and its contents belong entirely to City Cottage
www.citycottage.co.uk

Published by Little Knoll Press
First imprint – November 2014

ISBN No. 978-0-9927220-4-3

Copies of this book can be obtained from UK bookshops and from www.LittleKnollPress.com

Printed in Great Britain by Hobbs the Printers
Totton, Hampshire

This book is dedicated to Stan Bréhaut, (1921 – 2005)
whom Jack described as 'the finest outdoor cameraman in England'.
Stan was responsible for the filming of 1,000 *Out of Town* programmes.

Contents

Foreword by Fred Dinenage

Introduction by Paul Peacock

Chapter 1	A Country Boy	page 1
Chapter 2	The War Years	page 11
Chapter 3	Moving On	page 22
Chapter 4	Moving Out	page 32
Chapter 5	The Early Television Years	page 41
Chapter 6	The Out of Town Years	page 49
Chapter 7	The Boardroom Broadcaster	page 61
Chapter 8	High Expectations	page 72
Chapter 9	Ask the Experts	page 78
Chapter 10	A Jack of All Trades	page 93
Chapter 11	Jack Speaks Out	page 120
Chapter 12	Whatever Happened to Jack?	page 139
Chapter 13	Jack's Mail Bag	page 145

How *Out of Town* and *Old Country* were produced — page 153

Appendix: A selection of writings by Jack and others — page 158

Out of Town and *Old Country* broadcasts — page 172

Foreword

For me, Jack Hargreaves was, and always will be, 'the Guvnor'. He was the greatest natural broadcaster I ever worked with. Give Jack an old fag packet, a bottle, any kind of living creature - give him anything at all - and he could talk about it, unscripted, unrehearsed, for as long as was required. And he would always tell you something fascinating, something you never knew before.

He was also a top TV executive who gave me one of my biggest breaks on the long running, much loved ITV children's programme *How*, which still runs to this day as *HOW2* - and, yes, as I write, I'm still on it!

I last worked with Jack on a programme I presented for Television South (TVS) called *Southern Gold*, which looked back at some of the great programmes produced by Southern Television, in Southampton. We did a special programme in praise of Jack and his wonderful *Out of Town* series.

He was very ill at the time, but still bravely completed the recording. Afterwards I walked him back to his car, shook his hand and said, "See you soon, Jack."

He looked me straight in the eye and said, "No, old son, I'm afraid you won't."

He was, as always, correct. A couple of weeks later he died, shortly after his last television appearance on that TVS programme. I still miss him.

Fred Dinenage
2006

Introduction

The journey from Manchester to Birmingham should have taken about a hundred minutes, but already that Sunday the traffic was so bad that the six lanes of the motorway were jammed tight. Our steady sixty miles an hour had been reduced to only sixty yards and the excited anticipation of meeting with Simon Baddeley and his family, and Polly Boulter and her husband, was turning into a fear of being late. Polly is Jack Hargreaves's daughter and Simon is his stepson. It would be the first time they had met, and my wife and I were privileged to be a part of it.

Simon's house is crammed full of books and interesting artefacts. The front door seems to open into the real heart of the home, a passageway leading directly into a traditional and comfortable kitchen. A large table stands in the centre surrounded by well-used chairs. On the table there is usually a welcoming teapot waiting to fuel conversation, but this time we were late, there was no teapot, just a single pipe lying dormant on the table and a tearful Polly, to whom it had just been given.

*

It is remarkable how much Polly resembles Jack. She doesn't have a beard and nor does she smoke a pipe, but she has his eyes, his piercing look and his clear mind. It was much like meeting Jack himself, only she probably knew less about him than I did. She had become interested in her father from the day he had left her in the late months of 1962. She became known to Simon when she began buying up Jack Hargreaves items on the internet at the same time that Simon's wife, Lynn, was clearing out a number of items from their garage.

All through his life Jack had smoked the same tobacco, Gallagher's Honey Rub, so the pipe smelt inexorably of Jack. It had been one of his last, the bowl heavily scarred by constant use. It was a modern pipe, about which Jack raved. As Pipe Smoker of the Year, breakthroughs in smoking technology, such as a centre cooling spindle, had been important, but all this was now reduced to the effect of a single smell, a memory, an evoking of things now past.

Tea accompanied the afternoon conversation as the final pieces were put in place. Photographs of children on boats and in fields, on horses and with dogs and other animals, some perhaps not seen for forty years, were given their proper place. Many times, the words 'Of course!' were repeated as long missing pieces to a complex family jigsaw puzzle turned up, one after the other.

Slowly, a patchwork of Jack's life had appeared over many long months from the time I was entrusted with papers so meticulously saved by Jack's wife, Isobel. Some pieces of the jigsaw were still missing and would probably never be found but, if you stood back, you could see a pretty good likeness of the man.

Some of the gaps were significant; a number of important family members were not in the picture, and many of his friends mentioned only in passing. This is because this book is a portrait of Jack, the important influences in his life and the way in which he has influenced our lives.

Simon's living room was crammed with Jack's things and a good number of his own, collected over many years. On a shelf was a chub, beautifully carved in polished wood, swimming against an imaginary current, that had been taken from Jack's bedroom. He had loved the chub. He wrote in his 1951 book, *Fishing for a Year*, "It is one of the most excellent provisions of Nature that chub are to be angled for on hot summer afternoons."

"That was me on Hoppy, asleep in the bottom of the boat!" said Polly. The photograph was passed round and Simon said "Hoppy! That was *my* boat, she was wonderful." They were looking at a photograph of a young girl asleep on the boards of a boat that was full of various odds and ends. It was a picture of a happy day, one of those high summer days, the kind that children remember with joy from their early childhood. But these were two adults reliving two very separate childhoods and trying desperately to put them together. It was made harder for Simon by the realisation that he wasn't Jack's real son at all. Genetically, Polly was more closely related to Jack than he was. Since Jack's death, Simon felt that he was left with a part of his life taken away for ever. Now, of course, some of those moments had been replaced. Polly represented a piece of Jack returned to him; a new sister, and that was how he now introduced her to everyone.

More tea and more discussion followed. Why could the details of Jack's life not simply remain private, when he had often tried so hard to keep them hidden? Many heartaches are explored and personal difficulties explained in this book. In addition, there are numerous people to protect, as well as countless friends and fans who felt they knew Jack to be a certain kind of person. As the author, the task I had been handed was not insignificant; to write of Jack Hargreaves as a person, not an icon.

*

Beyond the motives behind this work, there are several rules that remain an absolute requirement. First, it must be true. It is certain that not all of the pieces of the jigsaw will ever be regained, but the ones that are here are authenticated and true and in no single instance has any reinterpreting of the facts taken place.

Secondly, this is an affectionate portrait of his life and outstanding achievements. His work in radio prior to the Second World War had been groundbreaking, so much so that he was widely known as a broadcaster before he ever went before the TV camera. The cover notes for his book *Fishing for a Year* state: 'Mr Hargreaves has a reputation as a broadcaster and writer on fishing.' This was in 1951, some eight years before the Southern Television programme *Gone Fishing* had even been conceived.

Jack's life and his generosity of spirit stand on their own merits. His humanity is perhaps an example to us all and, though there might be some who would wish to cast the first stone, it might be better simply to learn from him in this area in just the same way that we learn from him how to tie a fly or what a cock horse was.

That Isobel wished for Jack's story to be told is clear from the papers she kept. The order and the way she maintained them makes this apparent. It is a tale that all his wives and partners knew much of, but it was Isobel who knew it all.

Jack's greatest communication was not the countryside, not the changing of the world and not the way in which he was able to record the joys of country pursuits; it was himself. He was able to bring something of his personality to all his subjects, and it would remain impossible to understand him without knowledge of his past, however colourful and difficult that past might have been.

After yet more tea and discussion, out came mementoes of Jack contained in a couple of boxes. There were war medals, a huge chunk of solid silver as big as a fist inscribed by Southern Television, fishing trophies, pipes on plinths and brooches with hair in them, perhaps a memento to a long lost relative. They were Jack's and Isobel's lives collected in trophies and minor awards, and as such they marked the highlights from their thirty years together. The one award I was hoping to see was his OBE, but it wasn't there. Jack had always been confused about this award; he should have received it after the Second World War, but therein lies a story to come.

Jack's achievements are largely remembered as having been on screen, but this represented a small fraction of his life. He was so much more than *Out of Town*. He was a man just as at home in the Savile club, where he had been a lifelong member from 1944, as he was up to his waist in the waters of the River Allen, and yet over his life he was to become happier with the Allen. In later life he came to feel responsible for visitors from the town damaging the countryside which he made popular. Townspeople were bringing with them a very different way of looking at the country, and this was changing how the very fabric of rural life worked. Jack became keen to address some of these problems.

He even prophesied a future where this country would become a huge city covered in concrete with a countryside no longer used for food, but for leisure. How would life change for this country if we were no longer dependent on our own farmers for food? In part this may be the reason for this book, but to ignore my own memories of Jack speaking to me as a child from the screen in the corner of our living room would be disingenuous. It is this memory and this introduction to a world I had not previously known from my own Manchester childhood which leads me to admit that it is a celebration of this fond memory and the man responsible for it. Thank you, Jack!

Paul Peacock
Manchester 2006

When the Present has latched its postern
behind my tremulous stay,
And the May month flaps its glad green leaves like wings
Delicate-filmed as new-spun silk, will the neighbours say,
'He was a man who used to notice such things'?

(from *Afterwards* by Thomas Hardy)

Chapter 1
A Country Boy

In comparison with his contemporaries, Jack Hargreaves's childhood was one of middle-class comfort. He was educated privately and, in the days when few from Huddersfield were destined to reap the benefit of a university education, Jack's father was able to fund it for three children. Jack's father James Hargreaves worked for, and later owned, a wool manufacturing business. He was a successful businessman which gave Jack and his brothers a relatively well-to-do home.

Ada Hargreaves

His mother, Ada, was a milliner. Her major preoccupations in life were not unlike any archetypal Yorkshire mother of the time; the welfare of her family, their good name, bread on the table and a comfortable family home for her husband and boys. They were Methodists, which went some way to revealing their former poor status. It was the Methodists, along with the Poor People's Missions and Salvation Army, who welcomed anyone into church regardless of the quality of their clothing. Just a generation earlier they had provided education, food and the various legalities of life and death as the Methodist Minister was the only one trusted to read the contents of a legal document, a will or a summons.

The Hargreaves family was fortunate to have two homes, one in Huddersfield and one in London, the latter being used mainly for business as work required frequent contact with London wool merchants. The decision was taken that the children should be born in the affluent suburbs of the capital as midwifery was deemed to be of a higher standard in the south. It was also beyond a doubt that a London address on the birth certificate would have given greater access to career opportunities and James Hargreaves certainly had ambitions for his children. George Ronald (Ron) was born in 1908 in Eaton Park Road. He was to become an eminent psychiatrist. John Herbert (Jack) was born in 1911, and Edward Arthur, who became a doctor, in 1915, both at 48 Fox Lane in Palmers Green. At the time of both George Ronald and Jack's births their father was described as a commercial traveller, but by the time Edward Arthur was born his job description had become 'wool manufacturer'.

Jack's grandmother, Mary Jane Jubb
at her home in Huddersfield.
The house is still standing.

Jack's childhood was by no means idyllic. It was said that he hated his father and became wildly rebellious. Unlike his brothers, the relationship between father and son was poor, at best. Jack seemed unable to settle down, obey orders or even behave in a civilised manner and his father was simply unable to understand him. Toys would be thrown, windows smashed and every attempt to correct this seemed doomed to failure, resulting in yet more delinquency. The situation was exacerbated by his father's reaction to Jack, which he misunderstood to be proof of his dislike for him. Jack's brother, Ron, suggested there might be a medical problem. Psychiatry was often the only recourse for the middle classes to deal with unusual behaviour. This was still the age of family committals to mental institutions, and something prompted Jack's mother to see if anything medical could be done. In her desperation, she took Jack to see a psychiatrist.

The visit was of little benefit. Jack was an extremely unhappy child, and he did not respond favourably to being addressed by a stuffy old psychiatrist. He would probably have remained so if his mother had dismissed an inkling of something special she saw in him. Jack frequently spent long hours, even as a very young boy, wandering the lanes and fields of what has now become known as West Yorkshire's *Last of the Summer Wine* country, exploring fields and scaling hills.

It was this knowledge that brought her to believe he might enjoy a holiday on a farm. The family had a long-term friendship with a south country farmer and so at length he became a guest of a friend of the family at the farm of Victor Pargeter. This man was to become one of the key influences for a character referred to as the 'Old Man' in Jack's later writings.

He wrote of the 'Old Man' in both his books, *Out of Town, A Life Relived on Television* and *The Old Country*. He went on to explain that he was a composite of 'father, grandfather and uncles; together with old farming friends - in particular Victor Pargeter of Burston Hill Farm.' As much as Jack had disliked and rebelled against his own father in his early life, he grew to love Victor Pargeter. The holiday introduced Jack to a different world and a different routine. The dining room was replaced by the kitchen table and the comforts of gaslight, and then electricity, were replaced by the oil lamp, with hot water on tap exchanged for cold water from the well. For Jack it was a different kind of family life and it seemed to suit him well.

After a number of visits, it became clear to Jack's mother that he was happier away from home. This holiday farm became Jack's second home, and he later chose to consider it as the very heart of his real family. He seriously loved his mother and brothers, and his feelings towards them brought considerable guilt to Jack's mind, but something about the farm made him come alive. Here he learned about farming, milking, ploughing, shepherding, shooting and fishing, and it felt comfortable for him. He learned to catch rabbits and profit from the sale of carcasses at the weekly market, although he never really needed the extra income. He learned to set traps and nets, how to hunt with a ferret as well as a gun, how to skin an animal and how to respect the real life of the countryside. It was perhaps that he now had something to care for at the farm; he had chores, responsibilities and, critically, a newfound ability to think for himself. Ada came to realise in later life the value, in Jack's case, of the 'devil making work for idle hands'.

Young Jack ... after a good night out?!

Eventually the Hargreaves family had to draw in the reigns with regard to Jack's education. Much to his chagrin, the teenage Jack was sent away by his father to join his brothers at Merchant Taylors' School in London. As you might expect, Jack hated the experience, pining for his farm, and much of his teenage years were spent running away from school. He ran anywhere; into the cinemas in central London, into the countryside and to a local river where he fished. Holidays were spent at Burston Hill Farm whenever possible, and only then was he happy. It is certain that Jack spent very little time in Yorkshire during these years. He did miss his brothers and his mother, but not even these strong filial ties could take him away from the security of his farm.

*

Despite all his dislike for school, Jack was able to go to university and here, as in other areas, a family confrontation ensued. James Hargreaves wanted all his boys to enter the medical profession. Both of Jack's brothers did become doctors and, in their turn, they both married doctors. Jack, of course, refused point blank to do this, wanting to choose what he saw as a more practical way of life. Whether this was pure rebellion or an honest desire to forge a career of his own choosing, is not known. Jack's father insisted that he enter medical school, but instead he spent eighteen months at a prominent country veterinary practice as a pupil, in addition to working at London Zoo in order to gain further experience. He then entered King's College London as an undergraduate student in the Department of Veterinary Science.

At university Jack earned himself a reputation as a bit of a joker. His sense of fun and mischief were infectious, and he was always forging fun in as many ways as he could. Although much of his time was spent having fun, his studies were never less than satisfactory. His most famous jape was widely reported on the university grapevine and even made it into the newspapers. He arranged for the elephants at London Zoo to be paraded along Pall Mall and through the centre of the city, holding up traffic and causing havoc. His other notable achievement at King's College was to fall madly in love with Jeanette Haighler, a fellow student and the daughter of a Swiss banker. Their relationship progressed and they were married in 1932 when Jack was just twenty-one years of age.

Prior to his marriage, however, Jack would have to face some harsh realities with his own father. The downturn in world trade was disastrous for the wool industry and, although James Hargreaves had worked hard, the family business finally folded in 1931, mostly due to imported clothing flooding the UK, a lack of overseas orders, and competition. The British Empire had made a huge market for British goods and everyone around the world, desperately keen and businesslike, fought to produce products for the UK market in return. Consequently, in an attempt to accommodate international trade, the value of wool and woollen cloth in the UK hit an all-time low.

With the business gone, James could no longer afford to pay for Jack's education. Distraught, he travelled to London to tell Jack to his face that he would have to leave King's, his studies and any hopes of becoming a vet. For Jack this was no great problem. He was more intent on marrying, though he had not said anything about it to his family as yet, and to accomplish this would involve him in getting a job.

The meeting between father and son was more important for them both than either could have imagined. Jack was touched by his father's new humility. It distressed James terribly to let his son down and prematurely force him into the world of work. Many years later, Jack confided that he was broken hearted by his father's change in fortune; he did not like seeing him reduced to such a humble state before him. It was a moment of unity between them, which effectively brought to an end their many years of antagonism. After the meeting he began to see his father in a wholly different light. He was someone who now, in reduced circumstances, had found some great honour in his son's eyes and Jack did not forget it. There grew a strong bond of affection between them which was to last for the rest of their lives.

Quoting from Jack's curriculum vitae, written in 1974, we find out the following about his early career:

> "I was offered a chance to write technical material for Unilever Livestock Foods. This led to a move into writing and a long career in the media during which I have been lucky enough to work for very best of teachers. As a feature journalist for Christiansen of *The Express* and Phil Zec of *The Mirror*; in films for Alex Korda and Michael Balcon, in sound radio for Lawrence Gilliam, in magazines for the Hulton Press under Maxwell Raison and in propaganda for Sir James Turner of the National Farmers Union for whom I organised and developed the Information Department, founding The British Farmer magazine."

An old magazine clipping shows Jack on a radio show.

In reality, his first job for Unilever was to write copy for Spratts' Dog Biscuits. It was thought that his veterinary background would serve him well for the task. It certainly enabled him to understand the products he was selling. He said later that the ingredients in the dog food were such that feeding it to your pet was 'like getting your dog hooked on strong drugs'. However, he seemed to have the knack of writing good copy for the advertising industry. Consequently, his bosses were happy and he was persuaded to go freelance.

He also had plans to marry Jeanette Haighler. Her grandfather was an austere man who frightened Jack. He imposed strict terms on their marriage. Half a century later, Jack remembered the words said to him, in forbidding terms and with no room for negotiation, "You shall not marry my granddaughter unless you hold down a job worth a thousand a year!" This not inconsiderable challenge was met with alacrity by Jack, who never looked back after his entry into the world of paid advertising. Duly, Miss Haighler became Mrs Hargreaves and graduated from King's. Sadly, the marriage was not without incident. It ended in the mid-1930s after Jack had been unfaithful. His two sons, Mark and Victor, never really saw their father except on the television.

Their mother took them to the West Indies where she worked as a vet. They were reasonably happy for a number of years until ill health and a need for a proper education for the boys forced their return to the UK. Mark took a classical education and became deputy head of a private school in Bakewell. Victor went into academic life in France, eventually getting himself a doctorate late in life.

Mark, Jack's first son, recalled that his mother had a great deal of difficulty in getting money out of Jack in the early years. She took him to the local courts for non-payment on a number of occasions and was advised that her only option was to have him thrown into prison for default. She refused to do this.

*

Half a century later, Jack was to ponder his life in conversation with his stepson, Simon Baddeley. He considered it a strange thing that he could never put a foot wrong professionally, but his private life took a very different turn and was far from perfect. He wondered why the skills he brought to bear on colleagues and business partners, as well as people he came across from day to day, did not suffice in his home life. Jack said that his wives came to tell their children that any contact with him would be a disappointment to them. Jack was certainly not without blame in these relationships, but he could by no means bear all the responsibility for things going wrong every time. He was certainly no 'bounder' and he did love the women in his life. He was, however, captivated by the opposite sex and this led, inevitably, to a number of affairs.

Freed from the restraints of marriage, Jack thrust himself into his career, continuing as a copy writer with the prestigious advertising agency Colman Prentis and Varley and also entering the less predictable world of the theatre with stints at both the Windmill and the Fortune. The Windmill was well known for shows which included motionless tableau featuring naked women in poses which replicated some of the great artistic works and incidents of history. Amusingly, Jack was responsible for many of these showcases enjoyed, primarily, by men in the years leading up to the Second World War. It is perhaps interesting to chew this over while watching him broadcast in later years from his familiar shed.

While at the Fortune, Jack wrote a variety show called *Half an Hour to Play*. This, his big break, starred the popular entertainer Jessie Matthews, better known in later years as Mrs. Dale in the long running radio show *Mrs. Dale's Diary*. The show went out on the BBC and Jack was immediately poached to work in commercial radio, paid for at the time by sponsorship. With his commercial background, Jack was seen as ideally placed to provide new initiatives with products planned for inclusion in the programmes themselves, rather than the now familiar commercial break.

Anyone who thinks of Jack as being known for his television work in the 1960s and '70s may be surprised to know that he was actually famous before the Second World War. His artistic temperament, so stifled in his childhood years, was now allowed free reign at Portland Place, itself one of the most beautiful buildings in London and, in 1938, home to the Independent Broadcasting Company (IBC). It's branching staircases, galleried halls, frescoed ceilings and white gilt walls housed recording studios, offices, control cabins and mile after mile of wire. 'In the centre of it all is Jack Hargreaves's office,' wrote the Radio Pictorial magazine on April the 15th of 1938. It went on to say, 'And even when you meet him it is difficult to realise that this very young, young man, wearing a tweed jacket and flannel bags with the unruly head of hair and attractive, no-nonsense manner about him is, in fact, head of Universal Programmes Productions and responsible for eighty-six broadcasts a week.'

On moving to the IBC he had invented the Stork Radio Parade, a dance band programme recorded and directed by Roy Plomley, later to become famous for the long running *Desert Island Discs*, still popular to this day on Radio 4. They would again work together in the 1960s when Jack developed a radio programme which eventually became *Brain of Britain*.

One of Jack's great strengths was an ability to develop programmes which naturally appealed to the desired audience. "The first thing to think about," he told Susan Collyer, a reporter whom he greatly impressed, "is what sort of audience you want for the programmes. Then build the sort of bill that will appeal to them. If you have a product like Maclean's Stomach Powder, for instance, you want to reach an audience of over forties. Old-time Music Hall is designed to attract them. You see, our problem is not only to present entertaining programmes, but programmes that are also good advertisements."

Jack did produce highly popular, if unusual, shows. His Rizla Smoking Concerts were his most successful, more so than the Horlicks shows broadcast at peak listening hours. He was responsible for output lasting up to thirteen hours a day and viewed his job as producing a show which no listener would want to switch off once he or she had tuned in. Consequently, content was no less significant than signing the stars of the day.

To achieve his aim Jack personally wrote all the scripts himself and only when he was happy with the way the show was progressing would he pass on the task to a team of writers, even then maintaining a close eye on both rehearsals and production. This management technique goes right back to his early days with Victor Pargeter, a fact astutely recognised by Jack himself. The method went; watch me first, then do it with me and then I shall watch you do it until you are good at it! This responsibility rested on shoulders which were themselves only twenty-seven years old.

Following a visit to America he decided that he was unimpressed by the American take on product sponsored shows and felt that his own system was just as good. He was, however, very taken by a show called *The March of Time*, a news show so topical it had reporters hanging on telephones ready to receive news with the aim of broadcasting it the second it came in. He recalled, "News of the Hindenburg disaster came in after they had begun the broadcast, and before the show had finished they had put over the whole story - with sound effects." This instant, creative editorial style impressed him; it did not need planning, just a keen sense of what was right in broadcasting.

Jack's role in the heyday of the radio years placed him at the heart of much we take for granted in production techniques today. He introduced the hand signal as a means of communication while on air, using his finger on his nose to start a process and effectively stopping the process by 'cutting' his throat. His career progressed and, from making two shows a day, he became responsible for over eighty a week.

Although he had reduced his involvements in the world of advertising, one can only regard with some awe the super-human staying power and organisational abilities required to produce eighty shows a week and still work on a number of key accounts including milk stout for well-known brewer Ind Coope. One notable disaster, however, was Jack's line "The biggest development you'll ever see in trousers," a mistake which resulted in the recall of a whole print run of newspapers.

Chapter 2
The War Years

As with so many of his generation, the certainty of everyday life and the routine career path were interrupted in 1939 by the outbreak of war with Germany. Jack was called up into the Royal Artillery as a gunner and, like so many of his fellow countrymen, found himself in an arena completely outside of his own area of expertise. On the farm and in the countryside he had fired a shotgun and killed, but the requirements of war brought the burden of killing for entirely different and alien reasons.

Jack rose within the ranks of the Royal Artillery to become a bombardier and was then accepted for a commission into the Tank Regiment and a period of officer training at Sandhurst, where he came out top of the cohort. As a new second lieutenant, Jack pushed on into the new world of training men of how to drive and fight in tanks. He was very proud of the Tank Regiment and he excelled at the challenges it presented. He had an astute if not academic mind combined with considerable mechanical and practical skills. One of the Tank Regiment's tests of competence was to be able to strip down an epicyclical gearbox and reconstruct it in the dark. This was simplicity itself to Jack!

Early in the Tank Regiment his communication skills were called upon as he became involved in the mechanisation of the Guards, training them how to drive tanks. He believed this to be a move by the British Government in preparation for the end of the war. "We were all cynical about why the Guards were being given tanks," he said many years later. He reckoned, and there many around at the time agreed with him, that the Blues and Royals were equipped with tanks to enforce the government's will among the British forces after hostilities had ceased. According to Jack, the Guards could be depended on to fire at British Soldiers if they were asked to. After all, the mutinies that occurred after the First World War had been put down by the Guards. It was thought at the time that if there were mechanised units of the British Army out there disobeying orders, then it would be difficult for the government to deal with them in an effective way, and so it became important for the Royal Bodyguard of the Blues and Royals to be armed with tanks themselves. This course of action eventually had some hilarious consequences and much later, according to Jack, some fatal ones.

When Jack was a junior tank officer waiting for his own regiment to reform, he was sent to a special training camp to help train the Guards Armoured Brigade. After the mass evacuation of the British Forces from France to Dunkirk, the rush to rebuild an army involved the reformation of many regiments under new command structures and this took time. While they were waiting for this, the country was being protected by the Royal Air Force during what came to be known as the darkest days of the war. Jack, like so many other officers in dozens of different arenas, was put to work training; indeed, it was a likely probability that he actually trained Johnny Baddeley, the father of his future stepson, Simon.

During the Second World War Jack started out as a gunner in the Royal Artillery.

For this task they were given the Valentines, the smallest of all the tanks in the British Army. Tank men were traditionally quite small, and Jack himself was not particularly tall, but the Guards he had to train were huge men, mostly over six feet. Of course, the tradition in the Guards was for big, athletic men, with a certain ethos of do or die, but tank work was comparatively new and called for a different kind of soldier. "Their heads were always sticking two feet out of the tank, and they insisted on wearing their polished helmets, which the rest of us refused to wear." Jack thought it amusing that once the Guards found that something could be polished, they energetically did so, or painted it either red or blue, the colours of the Blues and Royals. This got the Guards into trouble with their equipment on more than one occasion. It was forbidden, for example, for them to polish the exhausts of their tanks; doing so would change the temper of the material and render it liable to fail, but the Guards couldn't help themselves. After a few hours of energetic polishing, all the exhausts gleamed as never before, but were ruined as a consequence.

Jack recalled that the sight of Guards in the tanks became an army joke. Furthermore, as an article of faith, a Guardsman had it drummed into him never to be parted from his rifle, yet in a tank there was never enough room for both. Despite all protestations to the contrary, they insisted on taking their rifles into the tank with them, making life inside most uncomfortable for no extra benefit.

After their training, the armoured brigades were reformed and it was to Jack's astonishment that "it was the Guards that were chosen to show their machinery and abilities to the highest-ranking officials and politicians in the land." At the staff college at Camberley, everything was painted and polished, and at length the Guards had to show off a manoeuvre in their tanks to no less a figure than the Prime Minister, Winston Churchill. None of their vehicles would start, because they had not done any vehicle maintenance, only polishing and painting. So the tanks had to be towed around the parade ground for them, with the Guards wearing their polished helmets peeping two feet above the turret.

Jack was too good a trainer to be allowed a combative position and in 1942 he was also recognised for his previous successes in broadcasting. Almost all the other broadcasters in the country had been reserved in their civilian roles to keep up the country's morale, but Jack somehow managed to slip through the net. His early enlistment into the Royal Artillery had been something of a disappointment to him and his eventual entry into Sandhurst may have been the result of some string pulling, as it is inconceivable that both he and the War Office overlooked his potential merits as a propagandist.

Instead of actually fighting in a war, Jack was given the task of developing forces radio, a new initiative in warfare designed to maintain good morale among the fighting men on the ground. Information, not tanks, would be used to keep soldiers on track. After the reorganisation of the army brought about by the British victories in North Africa, Jack found himself on Monty's staff. His job was to begin planning for D-

Day, making broadcasting an integral part of the plan to convince the Germans that the eventual attack would be further north than it actually was. This role as a staff officer gave him a good insight into what was happening in the war as he followed the army through Holland and into Germany.

Moreover, some of the stories of the Guards' push into Holland at the time of the 'bridge too far' incident, as told by Jack, point out some interesting failures, clashes of personality and shortcomings in leadership. Jack was involved with, and knew personally, most of the great figures of the Allied Campaign. He described Eisenhower as a great man who he had a lot of time for.

Jack and Bobby Bower, a war correspondent, had been working alongside the American General for some time. As the battle into Europe continued, Eisenhower's HQ moved along with it and his signalling apparatus, which was carried on five trucks and designed to give immediate contact with Washington or Europe, was moved along with him. This was under the command of a British signals officer, a Major known to Jack.

Bobby's job was to send back war reports every day, and these were collected together each evening and broadcast as a programme called *War Report*. One day, Bobby's signal set broke down and he went to the British signals Major to try to get it repaired. He was met with a blank refusal; the Major was busy and *War Report* was not, in his mind, a matter of great urgency. Bobby tried the Major a number of occasions and each time he got the same response. Eventually, he said that if the set would not be repaired he would take matter up with Eisenhower himself. "Oh yes! You'll complain to Eisenhower! Ha!" retorted the Major.

Bobby marched straight into the Operations Office and right in front of Eisenhower himself, where the Chiefs of Staff and various army top brass were poring over maps on a table, all astonished at the intrusion by this brash young man.

"Can I help you in any way?" asked Ike, then undeniably one of the most important men on the planet, permitting this momentary interruption of his saving of the free world by an upstart young and lowly reporter. After Bobby had explained his predicament, Eisenhower simply said, "Take mine, I'll repair yours for you." Within seven minutes the Major had been called for and Bobby had no more trouble.

Eisenhower, said Jack, didn't criticise anyone at all, he just got the job done. The Major was not in any trouble, he just had it made plain to him that he had some new orders to follow, together with a brief lecture on the importance of the role of the press in the running of any modern war.

Jack personally witnessed Eisenhower fire a General and put him back on a plane to the States within ten minutes of the misdemeanour. His crime was to call a British General a 'Limey Bastard'. Jack also knew that Eisenhower got on well with Montgomery and had a very high opinion of him. The two other major American Generals were Bradley and Patten, both of whom held Monty in considerably less esteem. Jack actually referred to Patten as a lunatic with silver pistols. These two were often openly hostile to the British, even in front of the press. They were scornful of Monty for taking so long to break out of his beachhead at Caen.

Jack described Monty as an awful man; "a frightful fellow, who was a genius at leading the ordinary man, in a Mark Anthony kind of way." Monty was sure that fighting a head on war with the Germans was not going to be blessed with success and had become convinced that the best option was to hit them with a left hook. There was no doubt in Eisenhower's mind that it was a good tactic, and so the British were allowed to plan the assault.

According to Jack's estimation, Patten was absolutely determined that he was going to be in Germany before Montgomery. He had almost mutinied over an earlier debacle regarding the liberation of Paris, where Monty had to pull Patten out of the area to allow the Free French the privilege of liberating their own capital city. The way to proceed with the war caused a battle at the very top levels, which was both intense and lengthy. In the end, Bradley and Patten were allowed to take the Germans on in a full-frontal attack, while Montgomery was to try his left hook through into Holland.

Monty had decided on an airborne attack, a bold move, not least because he didn't have enough trained men and he had to borrow some American airborne troops. At length they assembled a huge force to fight the battle of Arnhem which, at the time, was referred to as the battle for the three bridges. The British were to take the furthest and most difficult bridge. This huge effort was the biggest airborne assault to have ever taken place. "I have never seen so many aeroplanes in my life before or since," Jack said, recalling the morning of the battle.

A fortnight before the operation, a young intelligence officer friend of Jack's, Major Urquhart, was having a blinding row with 'Boy' Browning, who Jack described as the "biggest shit in the British Army." Frederick 'Boy' Browning was regarded as the father of the British Airborne forces, through his development of the First Airborne Division. He began his military career with the Grenadier Guards in the First World War and was decorated with the Distinguished Service Order and the Croix de Guerre.

Urquhart said the landing zones at Arnhem were unsuitable and too far from the objective. He wanted more observation flights, but Browning overruled him. He also had photographic evidence of good quality German tanks in the area, but still Browning would not give way. Everyone on the attack was told that the opposition had all been moved away to fight elsewhere, which they all found to their cost was incorrect.

Browning was reportedly worried that his Intelligence Officer might stir up trouble and he ordered his senior medical officer, Colonel Austin Eagger, to send Urquhart on sick leave because of 'nervous strain and exhaustion'. Of course, they flew off and the Americans completed all their objectives by taking the first two bridges. Everything that was feared by Urquhart about the British landing sites was proven true though. Not only did they have to fight against superior forces to reach their target, which was too far away in any case, but there were more German tank reinforcements in the area ready to join the fight.

According to Jack, his own Guard's Armoured Division had never fired a shot from a tank except in practice; he knew this because he had been involved in their training. "Europe was full of people like the 79th Armoured Division who had fought a thousand miles across Africa and five hundred miles up Italy and broken out of the beachhead at Caen, and consequently it was an astonishing decision that the Guard's Armoured Division should be given this job," he recalled. "Not because the Guards were not the bravest men in the world, because we all know the Guards are the bravest soldiers in the world," Jack said. "They were just completely lacking in experience; they didn't know how to fight with tanks."

They were to hold the bridge for forty-eight hours, but it took them longer than that to fight their way to it. Their path took them along a raised road with flat countryside all around. The single track road meant that there was only one way to travel; in single file. The Golden Rule of tank warfare is never to get yourself in a defile, which means avoiding situations in which you simply cannot manoeuvre out of the way. Every tank brigade has a battalion of mobile infantry and the Green Jackets were following the Guards that day. The Germans had an 88mm. gun. This was an anti-aircraft artillery piece that was especially adept at taking out tanks. They immobilised the first tank in the file.

In a later conversation with Simon Baddeley, Jack explained that the infantry should have been sent out into the countryside to deal with the 88mm. gun. What actually happened was that they removed the tank and sent another to replace it, which of course suffered the same fate as its predecessor. A single 88mm. gun was knocking out tanks for fun and holding up an army.

Jack blamed a number of factors for what became a nightmare. Certainly the Guards were inexperienced and simply transferred their traditional fighting instincts, however brave, to a hopeless situation. He also blamed a complete lack of co-operation from the air force. The RAF had Spitfires with cannons, but they were never called in for help. Eventually the boys at Arnhem were slaughtered by German reinforcements that were not supposed to be there in the first place. Jack said there was no doubt that the intelligence back at HQ had been wrong and that it was 'Boy' Browning, the Head of the Allied Airborne Army, who he held most responsible for that. Finally, if the Americans, such as Patten, had put enough force into the operation, then it would have been a success. Jack reckoned that Patten and Bradley wanted to prove that they "were the boys and Monty wasn't."

The Guards were undoubtably brave but had been shown to be somewhat inexperienced in their new role. Subsequent months revealed them to be quick learners. They were eventually to fight on into Germany with great success. Incidentally, 'Boy' Browning gained his reputation as 'a shit', to quote Jack, by reprimanding an officer for being inappropriately dressed while limping back from the front, all shot up and hot from battle. Jack was very assured in this opinion and he maintained that Browning, who apparently had his uniforms tailored in Savile Row, was more interested in himself and his own reputation than anything else.

He also swore that he would punch certain army officials for their attitude towards British tank soldiers. The tanks were extremely dangerous, and Jack was offended by what he saw as the reckless attitude of the army in putting men into American Sherman tanks. Since the Valentine tank had been brought out of service, the British didn't have a diesel vehicle. Being petrol, the Sherman, once hit, simply set on fire, burning its occupants in the process.

*

At the end of the war Jack was asked by the BBC, before his demobilisation date, to gather details of various battles so they could collate the film material they had from the various theatres of war. This would allow them to make archive accounts of what really happened. It was a task that would prove difficult to complete.

Jack had asked for a man named Percy Hoskins, whom he had known at the Daily Express, and they spent an extraordinary few weeks doing the rounds, trying to find out what happened in various battles in the war. One of them on his list was the battle of Cape Bonn, part of the second battle of El Alamein where the Afrika Korps had collapsed. Jack went to see General Peter Martin, who had fought in it alongside others while suffering from dysentery and living off two spoonfuls of porridge a day, directing his own forces from his tank. They were being told about the battle and during this discussion a head peeped around the office door: "No! You've got it wrong, Peter." It was the Chief of the Imperial General Staff, General Sir Alan Brooke.

"Damn it, Sir - I was there!" replied Martin, but Sir Allen Brooke sent for his PA, who was summarily dispatched to collect various maps and the story was straightened out. The point illustrated that you had to be a long way from the action, with excellent sources, to actually know what was happening at any one time and how a battle plan was proceeding. The closer you were to the fighting, the less you knew about what was really going on, and even a distance of a hundred yards, or a time gap of a few minutes, would be enough to change the ordinary soldier's, or indeed his highest-ranking officer's, perception of the events and why they were taking place.

From 1944 onwards, Jack was working in London in the Adjutant General's Department, headed by Colonel Wilberforce who had been a Don at Oxford prior to hostilities. He was working with an old colleague from the International Broadcasting Company, Dennis Griffiths. They worked in liaison with the BBC and some of the American staff on

Supreme Headquarters Allied Expeditionary Force (SHAEF), in particular Major John S. Hayes who had been Vice-President of Mutual Broadcasting Inc.

Their first mobile broadcasting unit followed the 21st Army Group, commanded by Major John Macmillan, who later became Jack's colleague on a number of television projects when, after the war, he became Managing Director of one of the then leading broadcast companies, Associated Rediffusion. The staff of the unit included Sgt. Gordon Cryer, the original producer of BBC's *Band Wagon*. This unit followed the war through France, Belgium and Holland, and on into Germany. Once in Germany, the Allies captured the Norden transmitter in Bremen and set up a radio station in Hamburg in a converted 'Musikhalle' which later became the home of Radio Free Europe. This would allow the British to transmit to most of Germany and into Europe. Here they recruited Corporal Cliff Mitchelmore, later to be loved on the BBC for various quizzes and programmes, and from then on a lifelong friend of Jack's, who would eventually speak at his memorial service.

Jack, along with other officers in direct command, had an amazing success on this European trip and pulled off what was possibly the propaganda coup of the war. The song *Lily Marlene* was not all that popular in Germany, the songwriters themselves having tried at least two dozen publishers before getting it accepted. It was eventually taken up as a signature tune by the Swedish singer, Lala Anderson, but was still not very popular. The Görings in particular hated it.

The song only became popular because of the RAF, who bombed the radio station that was at that time detailed to transmit programmes to the Afrika Korps. Almost all of their stock of records was destroyed and all they had left to broadcast to the soldiers was *Lily Marlene*, which they did, over and over again, for hours. When hundreds of prisoners were taken by the British in North Africa, they were all whistling the song, and consequently the tune caught on throughout Europe as the British pushed forward.

When Monty masterfully 'returned' thousands of Italian troops to Rommel, a gesture that was calculated only to slow down the German retreat, these men whistled the tune all the way back home to Italy. *Lily Marlene* was to become one of the very first pan-European hits.

When the Allied forces captured Hamburg, they also captured Lala

Anderson and when she was identified, Jack and his colleagues wasted no time in getting her to sing *Lily Marlene* on the newly created radio station, bringing homeliness to the propaganda he was feeding to the near-defeated German people. It was the first broadcast of its kind and was of critical importance from a morale standpoint. Lala Anderson was the German equivalent of our own forces sweetheart, Vera Lynn. The broadcast was akin to getting Vera to sing *White Cliffs of Dover* to a defeated British public, something which, thankfully, was not destined to happen.

*

The highlight of Jack's military career was to write and produce the evening's broadcast leading up to the announcement by the King on VE night. Jack decided to get a soldier from the Far East to introduce His Majesty, to remind people of the fact that the war there had not yet ended. The soldier waited around in London for three days, to be ready to make the broadcast at a moment's notice. Finally, he grew so bored that he wandered off to the pub and had to be retrieved by an army of frantic Military Police when needed for the announcement.

That night, Jack's staff car was stolen in the midst of general celebrations and was eventually recovered over eighty miles away, filled with beer bottles and one lady's shoe.

Jack left the army late in 1945 and returned directly to his civilian career, as though nothing had happened.

He was writing scripts for the BBC in 1946 and broadcast a radio play based on Popski's Private Army. In it, Jack revealed some of the life and work of Vladimir Peniakov, the son of a Ukrainian businessman who moved to Belgium. The son was educated at Cambridge and, in 1924, moved to Egypt to become the manager of a sugar refinery. The young Russian educated himself to speak all the languages of the desert as well as a number of European ones, and when war broke out he fought with the Libyan Arab Force, which eventually fell under British control.

Popski, as everyone called him, developed hit-and-run warfare and became as famous as Laurence of Arabia. He harassed forces and kept himself quite secret. Nothing Jack had learned about him from the network or army reporters and newspapermen was allowed to be broadcast during the war, such as the time when he took a garrison without firing a shot, stealthily creeping into the fort when a German soldier came out of the door in the morning for a stretch.

In actual fact, Jack thought him rather showy in a swashbuckling sort of way, but there was no doubting the feats he got up to and the appeal of the show to the listener, showing that even a six year interruption had not weakened his commitment to a programme no viewer would switch off once they had tuned in. Eventually, Popski lost his hand to a grenade and went to hospital asking the nurse to "clear up this scratch".

Jack's script was highly professional. It was broadcast on the Light Programme on the evening of 30th October 1946, at 8.00pm. The radio play resembled many of the comedy shows of the period, but this one was pure drama. One perhaps wonders why Jack did not continue with scriptwriting as a career after the war. Instead, unlike many of his colleagues, he virtually disappeared into the world of advertising, emerging only to make the odd fishing broadcast.

It is most likely that he was thrust back into the office world of advertising by financial motives. However, one last tale of his service years was kept secret for another twenty-five years. Jack was awarded the OBE in 1946 for his wartime service, but it was immediately taken away. This information was kept hidden by Jack until the time when he actually did officially receive the OBE for real in 1972. He and Dennis Griffiths had been asked to assist General Grover in preparing the final Honour's list for wartime service, and the General told them to put their names down for an OBE each. When the list was completed and circulated, the General received a ferocious attack from the Dowager Marchioness of Reading who thought that the Women's Voluntary Services (WVS) had not been sufficiently honoured. Jack's and Dennis's OBEs were taken away, along with a number of others who Jack thought to be more deserving still, so that some ladies from the WVS could be honoured. Jack thought it strange that General Grover manfully beat off some fifteen thousand Japanese but was no match for Lady Reading!

*

In 1944 Jack married Elizabeth Malvin Ernestine Fransen Van de Putte, the daughter of a Dutch Navy Admiral. They had met when she was working as an assistant in a recording studio at the BBC. Among the witnesses was Major P. Youngman Carter, the famous war correspondent and novelist. Immediately following the cessation of hostilities, the couple started a family, James Stephen Hargreaves being born in 1946 and Edward John Hargreaves in 1947. The couple sadly separated a year later. Their parting was described as acrimonious.

Chapter 3
Moving On

Shortly after his separation from Elizabeth, Jack met Barbara Baddeley. It was to become one of two enduring relationships which Jack enjoyed in the post-war years. Within a few months of meeting her, Jack had moved into her London basement flat.

Barbara Baddeley had married John (Johnny) Baddeley, a Guards officer, at the outbreak of hostilities. John is reported to have married in haste, as did many during those critical years, but the letters they exchanged show them to have had an extremely passionate early marriage. Johnny was keen to have children, and Simon and Bay were born in quick succession. Johnny was also a keen favourite of Barbara's family and was viewed as a fine catch; a Guardsman, an officer, university educated, good looking and, indeed, the epitome of every girl's dream. Clearly there was love between them, but somehow this faded as the war continued.

Johnny was badly wounded at Nijmegen and spent many months in hospital, during which time the final break up occurred. It is probably fair to say that they were incompatible. He didn't stimulate Barbara's intellect or drive her passion for life and, ultimately, it was she who left him. There had been a number of infidelities in the marriage, one with an American airman, Sidney Dean. He was an intelligence officer who ran bombing missions. After one mission he had flown over Barbara's countryside home and dropped a note from the aircraft for Barbara to read. Her son, Simon, still has the paper sixty years after it fell.

Johnny remarried into a very well-to-do Greek family with noble ancestry and, after a few boyfriends, none of them dazzling or special, Barbara met Jack Hargreaves. According to Johnny's new family, Barbara had visited Johnny while he was in hospital and told him it was unfortunate that he hadn't died, because it now meant that she would have to hurt him so badly.

Working for *Vogue* as a journalist, Barbara found herself rather hard up and needed to earn extra money. *Vogue* was one of those institutions which, at that time, considered the honour of working for them to be rather more important than the provision of an actual wage. Thus, unable to make ends meet on prestige alone, she decided to find a better paid job. After the war, Jack had returned to work as a senior editor and creative director at Colman Prentis and Varley, with many leading accounts, from cigarettes to foodstuffs. As Jack began his war in 1940, he had left the agency and the world of advertising behind but returned to it after the cessation of hostilities.

Barbara applied for the job as his secretary, which she got, and subsequently became his lover, although he was still actually married to Elizabeth. We do not know precisely what precipitated the breakup between Elizabeth and Jack, but it is clear that it caused her much heartache. It is apparent that she believed she could still patch things up between themselves, but no reconciliation was to occur. Distraught, Elizabeth would push her children up and down outside Barbara's flat, hoping to catch a glimpse of Jack with this 'other woman'. Whenever Barbara went outside to talk to her, she disappeared into the many surrounding anonymous London streets. When Barbara asked about the woman, Jack told her it must be his wife and that was the only explanation he ever offered. He lived with a strict maxim; 'Never complain and never explain'. He made it clear that the past was the past and that was how it was going to remain.

Jack moved into Barbara's flat on Christmas Eve of 1947, instantly changing all their worlds. In many respects he lived a very conventional English life. He was also full of energy and drive; a marked change from her first husband. Barbara recalled, many years later, that she was 'practically swept off her feet' by Jack's inventive fun.

Simon Baddeley recalls affectionately his own first 'encounter' with Jack on a magical Christmas Eve:

"It would be very personal for me, but because Jack became a particularly public person in his TV persona it is perhaps interesting to learn about the private person. There are no nasty secrets, but there are some rather interesting and intriguing elements to the story of his life. Jack was much more than the rather super person so many people liked on TV. I suspect he would have been difficult to live with in his younger days. I first saw him as this figure through a crack in the door of the Chelsea house we lived in for a few years in the late 1940s when I was six. I can still see (in my study in Birmingham) the set of wonderful Lydekker natural history books he placed under the Christmas tree for me that year - 1948. Some would have thought they were a bit old for a six-year-old – especially as he must have known very little about me. I love these eight wonderfully bound books for the fabulous ink drawings of every kind of creature. I look at them today - in my early sixties. Jack didn't even know I'd spied him listening to my mum, but I had wanted a sight of our Christmas tree all surrounded by presents - and that's when I saw this strange, large, dark-bearded man standing legs apart, hands behind his back, talking to my mum, invisible beyond the crack in the door. In those days both he and my mum were working for an advertising agency called Colman Prentis and Varley and going off to work in the morning to their West End offices on scooters.

That evening must have been the first occasion my mum had brought Jack home. He was then her boss. She had only just divorced from my father (but I didn't understand much about that in those days and had hardly seen my father ... away at war and then in Greece at the embassy there). What I remember of that evening was that it had all the engrossing magic so many children associate with Christmas - which I often still feel even now at that time of year despite the jading of maturity - but on that occasion with this strange, slightly scary-looking man in the house amid the tree lights and the multi-coloured decorations of that warm, carpeted room in Chelsea. I crept back like a mouse to my bed. I have no memory of Christmas day that year ... just that first glimpse on Christmas Eve of the man who was to be all but biologically my father.

I think I am the luckiest of men to have had Jack as my father, especially as many years later I got to know my dad and came to love him and his family too."

*

Not everyone was happy about the union. From the outset, Barbara refused to marry Jack, but once sure of the relationship, she changed her name by deed poll to Mrs. Barbara Hargreaves. Jack referred to the time at the end of the war as the 'Deed-Poll' age. Women were just beginning to live as equals with men, but divorce was difficult, and a divorced woman could certainly not remarry easily. Barbara, like many women of the time, simply changed her name, living as his common-law wife. She took the step of changing her name without actually telling Jack of her intentions. Thus they took it upon themselves to be married as far as the outside world was concerned.

Her family was violently against this; indeed, they had hoped that she and Johnny Baddeley would be reconciled, though this was never a possibility. Jack, in a taped conversation with his stepson Simon, recalled that the family had made it completely and continuously clear to him that Johnny was the real father of the children. In so much as Jack was left with the irrefutable impression that the children did not actually belong to him, he refused to take on the role of father. "They couldn't have it both ways," he said, pointing out that since he was constantly denied the rights, they could not force him to take on the responsibilities of the job of fatherhood.

Simon was at school at Ashford when his mother changed her name. The school secretary had told him in an almost nonchalant manner that his mother was now Mrs. Hargreaves, as though she had read it from the bottom of a letter. Their pretend marriage proved so effective that for many years he was completely unaware that they were not really married.

Simon and his sister Bay were to spend regular time away with their real father and came to understand the different ways the two families worked. Jack and Barbara's home was very conventional in many ways. There were family conversations, set mealtimes and decorum. Their father's home, with his Greek wife and other children, seemed wild and somewhat disrespectful. In a way they were happy in both worlds but found Jack and Barbara easier to live with.

In his sensitive way, Simon had problems with the dichotomy between his real father and Jack. He had difficulty referring to both his father and Jack as 'Dad'. Both men were important to him and he didn't wish to let either down or upset them. It was not just a mere matter of respect, but a mark of his real love for both of them.

Jack, from the time when he appeared at Simon's first and cruel boarding school to 'rescue him', had become something of a hero and a father figure. Over the years, Jack's relationship with Simon was probably the most important of his life, causing him to be terribly jealous of Johnny. Simon remembers mistakenly believing he had heard Jack swearing about Johnny Baddeley, accusing him of being a 'pseudo-gentleman', in a foul-tempered outburst. What Simon didn't know was that Jack had wartime dealings with the Guards Armoured Division and had his own reasons for his seemingly unwarranted outburst and generalisation that the Guards as a regiment were 'pseudo-gentlemen'. Only in later years did Jack have the opportunity to make it clear to Simon the awe in which he held theirs and his father's courageous tradition.

The anxieties Simon had about his own relationships with his two father figures were only to be worked through in later life when Jack was able to ease his worries. Although concerned about Simon having affectionate thoughts about his real father, Jack would not have wished it any other way. However, beneath the surface, the idea of Simon having a draw towards his real father probably hurt Jack more than he was prepared to admit.

As it happens, Jack made a fine job of surrogate fatherhood to Simon and Bay. He did his best to absorb them into his world, teaching them what he knew and exposing them to his experiences, passions and contacts in much the same way that Victor Pargeter had done for him, many years before. Their time was described by all as being joyful, full of fun and adventure. As Simon takes up the narrative describing his fifteen years with the partnership of Jack and his mother, it is difficult to avoid the comparison between this chronicle and Jack's dealings with his other children. With a true lack of information about what really happened between them, it is perhaps not safe to conclude that the personal skills, time and love that Jack lavished on Simon and Bay were somehow not available to the others. Maybe they were denied by forces outside of Jack's control.

Jack out driving with Simon and his pony 'Pewter'.

Simon Baddeley recalls again:

"We spent wonderful times in Scotland, Wales and elsewhere, and I hope I can convey something of the unalloyed joys of those times together at Hampstead, Midgham, Bagnor (near Newbury), Lymington and on visits to Exmoor, the Pembrokeshire coast, 'the wilderness' around Abergwesyn, the wet world of Snowdonia and highlands of Scotland.

Running through these places are memories of rivers, especially the Kennet, the Lambourn, and smaller streams like the Winterbourne, which ran through the garden of our house containing a postbox at Bagnor. It flowed into a mill stream directed by weirs that rejoined the Lambourn amid water meadows crossed by a footbridge. Later, for a shorter time, it was salt creeks and shingle strands edging the Solent. Also in this account are souvenirs that include magically inventive Christmases, parties, get-togethers and entertainments of our collective making. Between them, Jack and my mother gave Bay and me an abundance of happy experiences, whenever we were home from boarding school.

We enjoyed town and country. In London we would stay at one of the many addresses Jack and my mum shared; Edith Terrace in Chelsea, South Hill Park next to Hampstead Heath, Park Crescent Mews near Regents Park, Queens Street off Curzon Street in Mayfair, and then Montague Square, while travelling to and from a caravan in a field near the river Kennet at Midgham, then to Brook House in Bagnor, the place where I think of as having my childhood, and then Lofts, Lower Pennington near Lymington, where I first apprehended the relationship between Jack and my mother was ending. These places blended with visits to my grandmother in Essex and my great grandmother in Hampshire and their homes in London, to my aunt in the Highlands and, later, to times with my father, John, and his wife Maria and the Greek side of the family.

In London we roamed Hampstead Heath, free of oversight except for an almost constantly fretting childminder, until Jack and Mum returned from their West End offices. Later, when we all moved closer to the centre of London, we might still eat in, but would often go out to see a film in the West End (when you could still park a car in Leicester Square) and then have a restaurant meal, often at Bertorelli's in Charlotte Street, where our waitress was always Lily, who had known Jack when he ate there before the war. Later, when I was in my mid-teens, we'd go out to restaurants I came to know as rather special. We flew 'en famille' for a weekend in Paris, as well as to the Savile Club, to match being taken to the Garrick and other London restaurants by my dad. I recall enjoying all this, but also regarding it as normal. I didn't think we were especially rich or privileged.

In the country, Jack taught me to shoot, arranged for me to learn to ride, and took me out on many mornings to sit out over decoy pigeons, or go rough shooting on my own or with a group of his friends on Chamberlain Farm near Thatcham. He tried to teach me to fish, but while I loved trying to do it, I never mastered the patience or wisdom that fishing needs. My pleasure was sitting beside him on a bank, watching him and being given a running commentary; all this before he was talking about it on the television. Jack also taught me how to raise a tent and how to harness a pony for a trap and drive it. He made and taught me the use of my first fishing rod, my first air rifle and my first shotgun. He gave me my first 'expensive' bicycle, a Raleigh Roadster. He taught me the rudiments of woodworking, although I was undoubtably a bad student. He gave me my first boat and several that followed, including the one I sailed with a friend of mine, Sue, to Miami. At my request he taught me how to choose a good pipe and smoke it, how to enjoy wine, what made meat taste good, how to enjoy eating spaghetti and use chop sticks and recognise a good brandy and open and eat oysters. I didn't pursue the pipe smoking.

He also pointed me towards the work of classical composers he enjoyed, as well as popular musicians and singers such as Ella Fitzgerald, Rosemary Clooney, Ertha Kitt and Fats Waller. He loved reading and, again, moved comfortably between short stories, poetry, novels, thrillers and the rich literature of urban and country life, and knew his way around Marx, Freud, and Darwin, as well as Johnson, Dickens, Hardy, Dostoyevsky, Zola and a host of contemporary commentators, researchers and theoreticians of the modern condition, a few of whom he actually met. To understand something of war, he suggested I read 'The Red Badge of Courage'. I recall his enjoyment at repeating some of the catch lines of the comic characters in the strip cartoon 'Li'l Abner', and he loved 'Andy Capp'.

I think, when I was younger, I assumed he knew everything and cannot recall surprising him. Rather, he would suggest to me that I might like to read, view, have a look at so and so, and perhaps even meet them, which is how I came across various people with whom he had dealings in his work, and sat in on studio interviews and saw television at work or joined him for lunch with a policy wink from the NFU, or the world of journalism or broadcasting, including some of the celebrities he interviewed. I would be with him too on many of his early outside broadcasts, especially with George Egan and Stan Bréhaut.

When I was with Jack, unless the occasion called for patient quiet, the default condition was unceasing conversation about the world and its affairs. We talked at the table, when driving, when working at one of his numerous projects, both indoors and out, when walking or standing still. We talked about things observed, about history, philosophy, politics and religion, he anticipating the emergence of a new religion concerned with the environment in one discourse. When I was about sixteen, I learned, via riveting narratives illustrated on sheets of A4 paper, about great battles; the German advance to the Channel in 1940 and the debacle of Dunkirk, the North African duel between Rommel and the generals Churchill sent to fight him there, of Von Runstedt's breakthrough in the Ardennes and struggle to outflank the Germans at Arnhem, and most of all, the incredible story of D-Day and the Allied advances through France and Belgium. This habit and preference for constant dialogue was something I took for granted as how everyone conversed. "Intellectuals," he said, "are not by some normal definition intelligent. The words are confused. The thing about intellectuals is that they love, they are fascinated, by ideas."

Jack would talk with me, but also in every setting and company. I would hear him and my mother talking upstairs in our cottage and wherever they shared space that I could overhear. He also listened. The conversation was not one sided. He answered my questions, commented on my reflections, embroidered my theories, as he did with all the others whose company he enjoyed. He had a stream of anecdotes, jokes, maxims, recollections, observations, verses, quotations and songs - some ribald like 'Barnacle Bill the Sailor' which he'd sing to distract us on long car journeys, moving from deep bass to falsetto between Bill demanding entry at the door and the 'sweet fair maiden' promising to 'come down and let you in'.

Jack made many people feel good about themselves, adding to and embroidering rather than correcting or rebutting their understanding of the world. As I was with him longer, I'd hear things repeated, but this never palled. It helped that I had, over 15 years, come to share, sometimes unwisely, his good and bad opinions of others and to copy his view of pomposity and wilful ignorance.

If all this sounds too good to be true, it's because it was just wonderful until I needed to start making my own way in the world and my own mark, and there, I suspect, in retrospect, it was good that I went away to school for long periods of the year and was forced to do that, if even in the protected, but still sometimes dauntingly competitive, space of a privileged private education.

He wondered about what would happen in the world. "The thing I regret about dying is not being able to satisfy my curiosity about what's going to happen."

Although my emphasis here is on Jack, the memories I refer to are inextricable from the ensemble of the family of which he was a part for the years from 1948 to the time we left Bagnor for Lymington. These memories have kept their shine because of how I was looked after and loved by others before and after Jack played his wonderful part in our lives. This applies to this very moment and beyond."

*

It is certainly true that when Jack referred to anyone as his son, he was referring to Simon. In his writings and recordings about a son going to Cambridge, or his son sailing to the States or Europe, he meant Simon and not his other four sons.

Simon always regarded his relationship with Jack as something magical, and when the relationship between his mother and Jack came to its inevitable end, Simon was devastated.

The nature of Jack and Barbara's break up was complex. One outcome was that Jack and his secretary, Isobel Hatfield, became an item, but no one, not even Isobel herself, knew the full details of Jack's complex personal life. He did not want to have to live without Barbara, but he felt, yet again, that the circumstances had conspired against him.

Jack was clear about one thing; Isobel seemed to be unhappy in her relationship with both Simon and Bay, possibly because she was afraid of the closeness of their relationship with Jack. According to him, Barbara had never told the children the full and complex reasons for their parting. On learning this, Isobel felt guilty that she had behaved in a less than courteous way towards them as a result of what she had seen as their apparent frostiness, when all along they had not fully understood that her role had only been one small part in the many events that had brought about the separation. Isobel had been under the impression that once the relationship with Barbara was over, she would be the natural successor in Jack's life, but for some time afterwards, she had remained behind the scenes, hidden from public view. She was described by Jack as being devastated on learning that the children had not known the full details of the breakup until a family reunion some time later.

It was only after Jack's death that the situation improved, as Isobel came to rely on Simon for many things. Sadly, the same did not happen with regard to her relationship with Bay, which always remained at best rather frosty.

Chapter 4
Moving Out

Jack and Barbara's break up had its roots as far back as 1955 when Jack had employed Judy Hogg as a secretary to work from his home. The family had two homes in London, one used as an office and the other as accommodation. Miss Hogg was described as 'very beautiful with raven coloured hair and something of a fiery temper'. Having fallen for one secretary, Jack proved himself consistent and as a result Polly was born in 1957. Their relationship continued into the 1960's when Jack was a frequent visitor to the Hogg flat above shops in St. John's Wood. Polly has her own recollections of seeing Jack arrive in an anonymous grey van. His usual car at the time was a Mercedes.

A number of factors led to the break up of Judy Hogg and Jack. By mid-1962 she had started an affair with her new boss and ended her relationship with Jack. It was she who ended things and ultimately the decision left Jack with no regrets on a romantic level, although as a father he was angry to the point of fury that another man might be a central figure in Polly's upbringing. Furious rows followed, resulting in Judy's decision to leave Jack off the birth certificate, a step which would have made it difficult for him to prove his paternity as he was not Polly's legal guardian.

Jack wrote to Mike Brown, a lifelong friend and solicitor, requesting help in arranging for him to have guardianship of the child. Jack learnt that, in certain circumstances, one of which was the mother's willingness, he may have been able to take on the upbringing of Polly, but the major hurdle was broaching the idea with Barbara, something he mused on without taking action for a whole year, possibly wanting to see if Judy's new relationship would last.

It did last. She and her boss remained lovers for the rest of his life and when, after twenty years, he finally told his wife and family he was leaving them for Judy, he fell victim to a stroke and then a heart attack. Judy was left to fulfil a new role as nursemaid, and their remaining time together was marred by ill health.

After a year of procrastination, Jack decided it was time to raise with Barbara the issue of Polly and his affair. He did so and became more keen to push the matter further, which he would certainly have to do if he was to secure Polly a place in the Hargreaves's home. Speaking many years later, Barbara said that the issue of Polly's entry into the family would not have been a problem. What was now an issue was the apparent shift in Jack's behaviour; from this point on he ceased to be the strong, decisive man she had come to love and, despite frequent attempts by Jack to prove otherwise, she came to the conclusion the two could no longer live together. She said that she could not reconcile his desire to show her Polly's photograph with Jack's searching requests about guardianship and the new relationship in Judy Hogg's life and what this, in particular, meant to Jack, now the wounded and jealous father.

A further complication had also been the entry into Jack's life of Isobel Hatfield who was to form with him the second and final enduring relationship enjoyed by Jack, in this case lasting until his death in 1994. They had originally met when she worked as an administrative assistant for Beaverbrook Newspapers and again when she worked for *Time Magazine*. She was to become Jack's secretary in 1959 when she was described by Barbara Baddeley as a 'godsend' as it was Isobel who, through organisational skills and gentle bullying, enabled them to have money in the bank. This was, in itself, unusual; although Jack was very good at earning money, he was somewhat better at spending it! Isobel was fully aware of Polly as, being responsible for Jack's bank accounts, she had made the arrangements for Miss Hogg's maintenance payments.

Jack and Isobel's relationship went beyond that of employer and employee sometime during 1960. Her coded letters to him for weekend consumption were a part of a bigger picture of Jack's lifestyle. 'Friday special next week', when mentioned in the weekly letters to Jack, referred both to a series of work-related tasks which Jack had to complete over the weekend and also whatever else they might do to make Friday 'special'. 'I'll try to ring you after dark' was a warning that she was due to contact him at home over the weekend. Perhaps more intimately, when Jack wrote to her in his own typescript, she replied, 'Your typing is very good. I don't know what you employ me for. But then I do know what you employ me for!'

All this had become possible as a result of Jack's daily schedule. Barbara was leaving for work on Monday, often spending the whole week away, then returning for the weekend. The children, Simon and Bay, were both away at boarding school and Jack had a week of freedom. He revealed in later life that he had yearned for the security and simplicity of life with one single woman: a simple marriage with the old-fashioned demarcation of both roles and duties. He certainly did talk in more confessional moments of his regret that this had somehow eluded him in so many of his earlier relationships, but it was something he was finally to find with Isobel Hatfield.

Barbara, after the demise of her fifteen-year relationship with Jack, did have a couple of boyfriends before marrying Angus Burnett Stuart in 1965. They remained together for the last forty years of his life. He was a director of 'D. C. Thompson' and she moved to Scotland where she became part of the shooting and fishing set. She loved her husband but missed the almost impulsive way Jack would often take her away to do something exciting and unpredictable. She did meet Jack on a number of occasions before her marriage, but a reconciliation was never on the agenda.

By the end of 1962 Jack, who at the beginning of the year had had three close women in his life, was now left with one. It would be Isobel who would nurse him through his heart attack of 1964 and, with her vast secretarial skills, would simply organise a barrier around everything with a view to protecting him from family and friends, but most of all, from himself.

*

Isobel Hatfield was a prodigious writer, able to poke innocent fun at most things without offence, with an elegant and endearing style. Although she never actually made it as a writer, save for a few children's stories in the Christian Science Monitor, she relied on her other talent, efficient organisation, for her bread and butter. She became a secretary par excellence with a string of jobs in her inexorable march through the forties and fifties. Letter after letter in her own neatly collected papers proclaim the same statement, a genuine and heartfelt: 'We are sorry to see you go.'

Her father was a medical officer in the Colonial Service in Africa. He came from a long line of Empire builders who had become unemployed due to the fact that there wasn't any more Empire left to build. At the age of eight she was sent to Cheltenham, to boarding school at Rodine, and thence to Cheltenham Ladies' College. "My progress there was neither good enough or bad enough to cause any undue stir and I ultimately achieved matriculation with, to the amazement of all, distinctions in Latin and French."

On leaving education she was sent to Paris "with hopes of developing an unsuspected talent like a trial balloon, but the only talent that emerged was one for letter writing," and it was her racy descriptions of Parisian life which made her a real wit in her friends' eyes. Her parents, however, took a different view. Her letters talked of sexually voracious men, affairs, decadence and unrelenting Bohemianism. She was promptly and forcefully deposited into a London secretarial college and that was that. The trial balloon had burst.

She had worked in various offices until, in 1942, she joined the American Division of the Ministry of Information. She organised the visits of American journalists and, by 1944, she had joined FANY, the First Aid Nursing Yeomanry, now known as the Princess Royal's Volunteer Corps. She was posted to Special Operations in Italy that same year and stayed for twelve months, enjoying herself enormously. This work was sometimes difficult as their aim was to bring about a sense of normality following the upheavals of war. The brutal death of Mussolini, a desire for retribution and vengeance and a basic lack of food and the simple necessities of life, all affected her posting. She was, however, able to find time to see the sights of the country before returning home to be demobilised.

She had married Cyril Stephen Hatfield, an airman, in 1940, but like so many wartime romances, the relationship was brief. From the time of her divorce, and indeed right up until her marriage to Jack, she playfully called herself 'Hattie' in letters to friends and in some of her poetry. The break up with Cyril seemed to upset Isobel who wrote, '... when a job in the film industry offered itself as an antidote, I took it for three months and stayed for five years.' Her letters to her husband were returned stamped 'Not at this address'.

Following a series of cutbacks in the British Film Industry, she moved companies several times, including a spell at Ealing, where she worked on the film *Whisky Galore*. She commented, "Three months film making in the Outer Hebrides was a test of ingenuity and endurance to last a lifetime." Her career blossomed. She became a general assistant and then a production assistant, responsible for almost everything from tea breaks to film casting, and fell madly in love with John Gregson, the star of films such as *Genevieve*, but, of course, this was not reciprocated.

Reorganisations and closures in the film industry prompted her to move to Southern Rhodesia to head a typing pool in the Irrigation Department.

Her time in Africa was not always happy. She gained considerable experience in dealing with the locals; how to "be jolly firm all the time (and not all palsy-walsy one moment and then shout at them the next); explain everything minutely and be pleased with them when they're clever." White women were reputedly in some danger during the hours of darkness and did not go out, even in pairs. A friend of hers was whipped by a man who had been lurking in the shadows. She had been riding her bicycle home. Isobel developed a keen interest in the welfare and rights of the native Rhodesians, joining a club which raised money to build a nursery for local children, and frequently visiting the 'townships' built on the outskirts of Salisbury, which were home to the native workforce and their families.

Having not found happiness abroad, she returned to London to share a flat with a close friend and find work. Her father said that she should think twice about giving up a job abroad that brought in £50 per month to return to "this land fit for only miners to live in," though she surmised that this outburst had been brought on by the rise in the price of coal.

At this time Jack was working on *Picture Post*, but the disintegration of the Hulton Empire led to him moving to the National Farmers Union. Isobel had worked for both Beaverbrook Newspapers and *Time Magazine* which she had joined in 1956. She had made many friends, but was troubled about her lack of journalistic experience, and kept "bumping my head against a pay ceiling."

In 1960, Jack had been head hunted by Rosser Reeves, the iconic American advertising guru, famed for spearheading the election of Eisenhower in the early 1950s. At the time he was crossing the Atlantic every month to run both his own business in New York and Hobson Bates in London. He saw Jack as an advertising man after his own heart and brought him in to reorganise the creative department.

Whatever the relationship was between Jack and Isobel in 1960, it was he who pressed for her to be brought onto the staff of Hobson Bates as his personal secretary when he was made a member of the board. She was employed to head up the Creative Department Secretariat, but they were not offering enough money, something which jeopardised Jack's joining the firm. They offered her a salary of £660, over twice the national average in the UK at the time, but it was not enough to tempt her. Jack refused the salary and stuck out for over £1200. In a letter to the board, he stated that 'everything was agreed' to allow Jack to join the board, 'except the matter of Mrs Hatfield's salary.' It was indicative of his reputation in the advertising industry that he got his way. It was his networking skills, the people he knew, and his contacts, that made him such a highly valued commodity.

Their employment with Hobson Bates continued for most of the formative years of independent television as he organised the creative department into teams and actively worked on major accounts himself. It was at this time that she began effectively to handle Jack's most personal matters and, in many respects. Her protective instincts were probably the real springboard from which he was able to become the familiar broadcaster we now remember.

Much of their time together centred on Jack's work; she chose to remain in the background. Even Jack's family had to get used to a new regime. One day Simon had walked unannounced into the house at Lymington. He was left with a very clear impression that it was no longer his home. When Jack's brother, Ron, died in 1965, his widow Sylvia packed the children into a caravan and headed straight to Jack's home. She recalls that she was made to feel most unwelcome by Isobel, an experience which took some years to heal. Isobel often gave the impression of being a starchy company secretary intent on restricting access to her boss, which was exactly what she was doing.

This role marked much of her life with Jack. Family, friends and business people were treated alike, a kind of universal board meeting to be arranged, minuted and organised. The consequence of this seems to have been to keep the world at arm's length. Mark Hargreaves, Jack's son by his first wife, wrote in letter requesting a meeting, '... although I don't feel I have been a very suitable son for Jack, spending most of my time indoors with music and the written word, Susan (Mark Hargreaves's wife) comes, on her mother's side, from a long line of Norfolk farmers.' He continued, 'Do I dare ask whether I may look in on you on Monday 27th? I have nothing to ask of Jack - except the book ...' Of course the meeting never took place. Jack was ill with heart problems at the time.

His brother, Victor, also wrote to Jack on the event of his engagement, as notified in *The Times*. He thought it best to telephone Jack's office and explain that he might be in the newspapers. He was surprised to have the telephone answered by Jack himself - something he found very embarrassing. 'I am sorry,' he wrote afterward, 'I did not realise I would be talking to you directly ...'

The television programme *Out of Town* was eventually to lead Jack in many new directions. In addition to the hunting, shooting and fishing world in which he always seemed comfortable, he felt he simply had to become a farmer. Until this point, Isobel had been the quintessential cocktail housewife. At least one of her friends seemed to recognise the change in her. Elizabeth Nel, writing from South Africa in 1969, commented:

'You sound wonderfully happy and long may that state remain. I can hardly picture you with capacious apron and dripping face bending over a hot-pot, beating up innumerable seed-cakes á la Mrs. Beeton, or grubbing in the garden to grow your own sweet williams; rather sitting in tight black slacks before one of those roaring Dickens-type fires in a huge fireplace, smoking a cigarette in a long holder and discussing dynamics.'

Clearly life with Jack changed Isobel. Among her effects and papers left behind after her death in 1997 were a good number of cook books, hundreds of handwritten recipes, knitting patterns, dress-making books; in fact every evidence of what might be termed the 'traditional' feminine domestic life.

She and Jack did remain happy. He was away a lot, filming with cameraman Stan Bréhaut, buying stock for the farm, or simply fishing and shooting. Isobel was his home and he returned to her night after night, week after week, contentment written into his daily life like a script. Clearly there were some regrets in Jack's mind, but there was always fun, sometimes understated fun, sometimes remembered fun, and not more so than when he spoke with Isobel. His pet name for her was 'Frog', a name which had its origin in the following letter.

```
The Pond,
The Bush,
London.
W11.

6th September 1963

Dear Mr. Hargreaves,

     I never miss your programmes and, being a
town-dweller by force of circumstances, I greatly
```

enjoy the breath of the countryside that you bring to Channel 9 each Friday. My only complaint is that it is All Too Short.

But I have been greatly disturbed by this evening's programme and I feel I must protest, on behalf of all frogs everywhere, about your suggestion that frogs should be used as bait.

You seem a very kind man, and I am sure that it is only thoughtlessness, not cruelty, that leads you to give publicity to such a terrible idea. Frogs have mothers and fathers and brothers and sisters and husbands and lovers and things like anybody else. And how would you like your nearest and dearest to be eaten by a bass? Or pike? There may be boys all over the country even now going out with their frogging nets to catch thousands of Us to use as bait tomorrow (Saturday), causing untold suffering among my friends and relations.

Please, Mr. Hargreaves, use your influence to put an end to this dreadful practice, both here and in the U.S.A. Porkrind or genuine frog-flesh, it makes no difference.

Yours very faithfully,
A Frog

Isobel and Jack shared a keen sense of fun which, together with the love and respect they held for each other, enabled them to spend the next thirty-four years together; perhaps the ideal Jack had spoken of when musing over earlier, less enduring relationships. They were often apart because of work commitments, but the rest of the time they were inseparable. They travelled widely; France and Spain, America and the Far East, each trip carefully chronicled for television programmes.

Sadly, their relationship was not blessed with children. A medical problem following surgery in Rhodesia had made that impossible for Isobel. Consequently, she threw herself into the task of running Jack's affairs and acting as hostess to numerous visitors, many of whom wrote to thank Jack for his time and Isobel for her wonderful food. She always replied with a personal note.

What Jack referred to as their "modest times of comfort," by which he meant financial security, was the result of Isobel's efforts. Among the papers she kept there was every electricity bill, every rates demand and every cheque stub and receipt. She managed the household with remarkable efficiency.

Throughout her life she had always been worried about her old age. She had wanted to be married and settled and her years with Jack were the happiest of her life. The quiet tick of the clock, after Jack's death, was to haunt her final years and her own old age was passed in organising the remnants of her husband's affairs and pondering the long and treasured adventures they had shared.

Chapter 5
The Early Television Years

Jack's return to Colman Prentis and Varley after the end of the Second World War had been as smooth as if the war had never taken place. He worked on their best accounts; Shell 'Keep going well', B.E.A., McDonalds Biscuits, Goya Perfumes, The Conservative Party and a number of Hulton Press accounts. Jack's work with the Conservative Party had been one of the first forays of a political party in the UK into the world of public relations and market research. It had been this move into political PR which had brought Jack to the attention of Rosser Reeves and was ultimately to lead to his involvement with Hobson Bates.

Jack did not return again to broadcasting for the IBC, but his then role as librarian of the Piscatorial Society did lead him to making several radio programmes for the BBC on fishing, which eventually became a book, *Fishing for a Year*. The title was undoubtedly a dig at those people who engaged solely in one aspect of the sport. Jack felt that anyone engaging in, for example, fly fishing should also pit their wits against pike or barbell. He viewed a year as perhaps sufficient time to engage in all aspects of the sport.

Jack also began writing for various newspapers, often on country matters; by now he had become widely known among fishing syndicates and shoots around the country. He also wrote about other subjects such as motoring or, more infrequently, travel or the war. He wrote mostly for the *Daily Mirror* until he moved, in the early 1950s, to work full time for the Hulton Empire, a move which came about through his friendship with the writer and broadcaster Patrick Campbell. They had both become regulars in a number of Fleet Street public houses. Their ale-house friendship was frequently raucous, and they would sing, play games and generally have a good time.

*

Patrick was one of those people who knew everyone and would drop his friends a tip or two about media jobs due to become available, even before they had been vacated or advertised. As a result of numerous such tips Jack joined *Leader Magazine* as an Assistant Editor, *Lilliput* as

Editor and later, having passed this baton on to his friend Collin Willock, he became Managing Editor of *Lilliput* and Editor of *Picture Post* in its final years before the closure of the Hulton Empire.

Lady Hulton had taken over the reins of the publishing empire from her sick husband. She had been a refugee to the West, a princess escaping from the Russian Revolution. She had obtained a position as a secretary in Lord Hulton's office and eventually married him. Her aristocratic aloofness was legendary. It was in his dealings with Lady Hulton that Jack began to lose the awe in which he had held the nobility. He had previously mixed with minor nobles from his army days onwards and had been a member of the Beaulieu shoot. He had also been a member of the Savile Club and had been flattered by the attentions of people of rank.

Jack out shooting, probably on the Beaulieu estate.

Lady Hulton amused Jack. She would 'receive' her editors in the manner of a Dowager Duchess. Frequently Jack and his colleagues were escorted to her bedroom, where she addressed them in various states of undress. Jack believed she did not mind talking to servants and other various 'minions' in this manner, because their opinions and lives were so beneath her for it to be of no consequence that they viewed her with no clothes on. It was an extreme show of nobility at the expense of the personal niceties which made up normal society.

When she called into the office, she would use the gentlemen's toilets and, when it was pointed out to her that it wasn't 'the done thing', she simply pointed out that it was she who paid for the toilets and she would use whichever ones she preferred. Lady Hulton also had a habit of sitting under the clock and stationing her chauffeur in such a position that he could tell her the time, thus avoiding the need to turn her own head for the purpose.

Hulton had wanted to go into television and Jack, with his contacts, had been asked to carry on his job as a director so that he could help them gain and operate a television licence. But in the months leading up to the demise of the Hulton Empire the firm began to haemorrhage senior executives, Jack among them. He had made the decision to enter television in his own right.

Lilliput was sold on the break up, to become *Men Only*, and *Picture Post* disappeared altogether. Jack moved on to the Institute of Directors to make a series of television programmes called *Enterprise*. It took a year to produce them and during this time Jack formed a production company, T.V. Advertising (TVA Ltd) that was to take on the filming. They were all set to schedule the programmes on air. Both the Institute of Directors and Sir Robert Fraser, the initial contractor, were happy with what they had seen, but an attack from government brought the scheme to a halt and the programmes were never broadcast. TVA Ltd. began to make commercials for some of Jack's Colman Prentis and Varley clients. Jack was one of the company's two directors.

Late 1957 saw Jack move to the National Farmers Union (NFU) as Director of Communications. His work involved monitoring television and radio broadcasts as well as inspiring their production, something he had become adept at doing during his involvements with propaganda at the end of the Second World War.

Jack at his desk at the National Farmers Union.

Sometime during 1958, Southern Television had put out a programme on the subject of meat marketing that was viewed by the NFU as wholly inaccurate. Jack was dispatched by the president to take the company to task about the dubious content, and he spoke to Roy Rich, a great innovator during the early years of Southern Television when the main focus of their output was regional material, much of it rural in nature due to the audience.

At that time the bulk of farming output was under the control of Arthur Street, who Roy described as a 'hardheaded farmer'. He was also responsible for all broadcasts dealing with rural issues. To our eyes the programmes they ran would have seemed rather formal and stuffy, with Roy Rich himself seated before a rattan or willow fence in a studio setting where he would discuss topical issues with well-dressed farmers who themselves would have seemed more at home passing the port in a gentlemen's club.

The then owners of Southern Television were well known to Jack, who was probably as much at ease in the boardroom as he was in the field or by the river. One quarter of the shares were owned by D.C. Thompson, the Scottish publisher of magazines and comics. The rest were owned by Associated Newspapers and The Rank Organisation. It is interesting to note that within five years of Jack making his first programme for Southern Television, his partner of fifteen years, Barbara Baddeley, married the Chief Executive of D.C. Thompson, Angus Burnett Stuart.

Roy Rich was determined to generate a wider appeal for Southern Television, and he had gathered around him a two hundred strong team to achieve it. Together they had made a number of groundbreaking and memorable programmes, paving the way for much of what was to become Independent Television. In its earliest form, though, Southern had given the impression that it was content to sit in the background while richer broadcasters in London and the Northwest led the way. They had found it difficult to get their own programmes syndicated to the other broadcasting companies which formed Independent Television (ITV), their reputation being that of a small, regional relative with a rather parochial output.

Faced with Jack's criticism of the nature of their farming output, Roy Rich really only had one option; he hired him and they lunched together at Scott's in Piccadilly, where he commented that there were a lot of fishermen in the Southern Television region. "There should be," Jack replied, "because you have some of the best waters in the whole of the UK."

Roy had been toying with the idea of a fishing programme to capture this huge market. Jack thought it would be impossible. Fish could not be caught on demand and the cost in wasted film would have been as prohibitive as the intervening hours would have been boring. He also felt, quite perceptively, that a further problem would have been the thickness of the line; the camera would have found it impossible to pick it up, especially given the quality of early VHF transmissions so it would have seemed to all and sundry like a man waving a bendy stick in the air.

Roy would not let go of the idea. One reason for this was the regional popularity of fly fishing, then universally a rich man's sport. It was pretty much the realm of the company director but, as Roy reasoned, these were the chaps who were their potential advertisers. Thus, despite the practical problems they would have to overcome to achieve it, the production of a fishing programme became inevitable.

It was Roy Rich's plan to break the mould of studio based programmes and Jack's insistence that "there must be something better" that made their success a certainty. This was a challenge, not a threat to their plan, and Jack's experience of mobile field reporting from the war had made him the ideal man to improvise a new kind of television broadcast; the outside broadcast (OB). His old friend Roy Plomley from the Stork Radio Parade on the IBC had developed the art of OB in the early days of commercial radio and Jack had a few more tricks up his sleeve. At that time, shows filmed outside the studio had been done before, but no one had even considered making an entire series that way.

*

As a first step in his television career Jack was asked to work on *Farm in the South*, a rural interest programme dominated by Arthur Street. As the story goes, Roy wanted Jack to catch a fish live on the air and to capture this a huge OB unit was set up to cover the event. Jack was not convinced it would work; what if nothing was to bite? It could have become an exceedingly boring flop. Of course it didn't and Jack became the very first man to catch a fish live on television. 'Come and do six fishing programmes for a lark,' Roy Rich wrote to Jack. Thus *Gone Fishing* was born in 1959.

Fly fishing in the summer.

In later life, Simon Baddeley described Jack as a somewhat atypical fisherman. There are many who could not appreciate a landscape except as a setting for hunting, shooting or fishing. Jack was not one of them. He could communicate even the tiniest nuances of a landscape and any fishing lesson became not just that, but also a lesson on cloud movement, on wind or how fish in turn swarm as a consequence. He would notice a water rat and have an appropriate tale about its habits. There were no boring silences as you waited for a brown trout or a grayling to bite. Every riverbank, every field and all the life which inhabited them became an inspiration to Jack. He was in his natural element. All those trips into the country, his years of study and those few short, valuable years at the Pargeter Farm came into sharp focus as Jack came to realise he could communicate the tale of the countryside as though it was his own personal history.

The first programme in the *Gone Fishing* series dealt with fly fishing. Jack went with a Southern Television cameraman called Georgie Pellet, who shot him casting a floated line in the mill pool at Fordingbridge, on the River Avon in Hampshire. They then went into the studio and, with the use of a barrel filled with water, they demonstrated how a float behaved as it bobbed up and down on the surface.

The *Gone Fishing* series invented a whole new way of producing a television programme. There was a single cameraman, a single director and a voice over. The programmes were broadcast in late spring and in their day were not merely the mould breakers Roy Rich had intended, but rather the creation of an entirely new format. Jack knew from his days in advertising that although viewers might have been numbered in the thousands, his role was to communicate as though to just one; an intimate and cosy style very much in the manner of someone sitting on the sofa next to you. The shows were a quiet chat with a respected and expert friend.

Even now people remember him as 'their' Jack for precisely the same reasons which made those early broadcasts such a success. It was a sense of 'Jack and I went fishing' or 'he took me out to some river to share his passion for the lore of fishing and the satisfaction of a well landed trout'. So successful was the format that they followed up the first six shows with a further twelve. In total they made twenty-eight shows with Jack earning fifty guineas per programme.

Late in 1959 Roy Rich took Jack out to lunch. He wanted to continue with the show; viewers' letters certainly confirmed that they were hungry for more. Jack, however, felt that they had covered the subject of fishing. "It seems to me," he said, "that people think they have been able to get away from town, and that's why they like it. You can do anything you like as long as you are a very long way away from town."

In late January, Roy Rich wrote to Jack to explain that *Gone Fishing* was to disappear from the schedule. A new programme list had been agreed with the Trade Union with the result that there would be no room for any further series. Roy promised to try to get it back on the air as soon as he could but refused to commit as to when it might be. With his television career coming to a possible end, it was left to Jack to convince the programmers that he was as essential to the future of television as he had been to both radio and the advertising industry.

Responding to the challenge he produced three one off outside broadcasts. They were so good they prompted Roy Rich to write the following communication on the eleventh of February:

```
Dear Jack.

     Well done, thou good and faithful, I was
delighted with you and watched all three of your
inimitable contributions.

     I had already arranged a meeting with Jackie
Jackman to sort out a return date for you, but
I've gone a bit further than this now and suggested
to Berkley that we fit in three or four more of
these OBs. You appeared to be enjoying yourself
sufficiently to encourage me to think that you
would like to do a few more? In the meantime, I
have asked Berkley to contact you direct.

     Southern, and me, are delighted with you.

                    Yours sincerely,
                    Roy Rich
```

A new kind of country programme which dealt not only with fishing would need a new name. Roy Rich produced a series of sentimental prospective titles such as 'And Far Away', but Jack wanted to avoid that view of the countryside. In fact his ideal title was overheard on a train as spoken by some upper-class ladies who were talking in a loud and rather irritating manner. "I couldn't possibly come to dinner on Friday," said one to her friend, "for we shall be out of town." The last three words struck a chord with Jack and thus one of the more familiar names in television history was born.

Jack telephoned Roy Rich. "We're going to call it 'Out of Town'." Roy did not like it but deferred to Jack's instinct. "It's too ordinary, but if you think you must, you must!" Now with a title the programme needed a cameraman of extraordinary ability to pull the whole thing together.

Chapter 6
The Out of Town Years

In 1959 Southern Television opened their Dover studio and Georgie Pellet was made head cameraman. Jack was introduced Stan Bréhaut. It was the start of a strong partnership and they were to work together for the next twenty five years.

Prior to the *Out of Town* series, much output broadcast on television seemed to be based on the music hall principle. Jack's show was one of the first to use a down-beat though beautiful piece of music as the opening credits first screened on July the sixth 1960. The piece Jack chose was a version of *Recuerdos de la Alhambra*, composed by the classical Spanish guitarist and composer Francisco Elxes Torrega in 1899. At a cost of seventy pounds he commissioned a recording for use solely with the programme, complete with the recognisable lilting rhythms which would introduce the series for a quarter of a century.

Jack and his pack pony 'Ghost'- the opening sequence of each programme

Jack had never heard the original and swore that the group, whose name sadly seems to be lost, had both composed and recorded it in the late fifties. Stan Bréhaut, however, was a musician. He played the guitar, had built his own instruments and had played in a band for many years. He even had a version of the record by the great Segovia on an old record at home. On hearing it Jack had to give way on this. Stan commented that this was one of the rare occasions they had disagreed.

Later, in 1979, Jack said that they had worked together for twenty years without a single cross word; probably something of a professional record. Jack needed a unique style of filming to achieve his personal vision of what the programme should be and Stan Bréhaut seemed to understand this. They became a team and were very much united in their approach to work. Instead of a huge entourage of technical people there was simply the two of them. Stan wrote:

> 'My wife and I were the local photographers, using a couple of Hasselblads, a wide-angled one and a PIM monorail technical 5x4 plate camera, and plenty of lenses for both. When Southern TV opened here, I also had a cheap 16mm fixed lens film camera, and because I was the only option, I became employed as a freelance film cameraman. I had never been taught how to use a movie camera, so I made it up as I went along.'

Stan brought a photographer's eye to movie shots. He kept the camera motionless, simple filming considered best for the job. There were very few pans or special effects in the early programmes. It became such a natural and intimate style that the audience could not help but feel that only Jack was there by himself. Stan often cited another Stan, Stanley Kubrick, as an influence, in that both had started out as photographers and had then worked on documentary shoots early in their careers but, while Stan had remained with Jack making *Out of Town*, Stanley had gone off and found international fame.

Stan worked on all the original *Out of Town* series. He was also the cameraman on *Country Boy* and 'Freewheelers', a children's adventure series. He admitted to being quite ignorant about country matters and wildlife in particular. Rather than regarding this as a hinderance, Jack actually put it to good use. He believed that if it interested Stan, it would interest his audience too and he should shoot it. Jack's comprehensive knowledge of nature would lead him to overlook a lot of material as commonplace, but if Stan found it of interest or felt he needed to know more, it would probably be regarded in a similar light by the average viewer. Stan said they became a 'quiet duo', with neither needing much in the way of direction.

A young Stan on location with Jack.

The name Bréhaut has its roots in the Channel Islands and his family had been fishermen and blacksmiths. His father had come from Guernsey to Eastleigh in Hampshire to work on railway engines at the turn of the century. His grandfather and great uncle were still sea fishing with a boat at the age of 90 and 91 respectively. They had done so by both traditional and innovative means, using white knicker elastic as a lure. When one of the brothers died, it took a huge effort by the remaining family to persuade the other to stop going out fishing.

Jack was on record as saying that Stan was the finest outdoor photographer in England and a tremendous technician. He also made his own equipment and adaptations for his cameras, such as a huge aperture ring, about the size of a saucer, which allowed him to read off his aperture for the lens with one eye while using the other to frame the shot in the viewfinder. Of course, this was in the good old days of wind up cameras with no electronics or automatic exposures.

It was pigeon shooting sequences that Jack believed showed Stan to be the complete and consummate cameraman. When pigeons arrive overhead, they come in numbers of around half a dozen together and they travel fast. Jack would shoot one of them, but Stan could not know which one it would be.

"The right one!" Jack would shout, but, as he said this, the bird would cross to the left, leaving a frustrated Stan stuck filming the right. They tried many times, but the task seemed impossible. Stan, however, did make it possible. He built an open viewfinder for the camera, with the result that it was not necessary to bring it to the eye straight away. He picked out the bird in his invention and then transferred it to the viewfinder; this being the most difficult part of the operation. Stan said he needed something that would fit in between the open viewfinder and the camera eyepiece to make the shot right. He set to work on yet another invention.

Jack had an old German sniper's sight he had found and brought back from the war. Stan mounted it onto the camera. This allowed him to capture the shot perfectly and he was able to use it in the following sequence: open viewfinder, sniper sight, then camera viewfinder. This enabled to catch the bird in mid-air. And yet, if it was flying quickly towards Stan, it would become blurred, so he would have to pull the focus back continuously. On being shot by Jack, the bird would then fall down, away from the light sky and against the dark woods, which meant that the exposure would change again. Stan would then have to pull the aperture as well as the focus.

Jack was amazed when they started filming together that Stan didn't know a single bird's name. Even after twenty years of continually working in the countryside, and after Jack had told him time and time again the names and behaviour of each bird, he still only knew a handful by name. His sole interest was in getting the shot right. Once, they filmed two of the rarest small mammals in England. A naturalist friend in Wiltshire had found a squirrel tailed dormouse and a yellow tailed mouse. These were regarded as being so rare that many people had denied their existence in the UK. About a week after shooting they were talking to someone in the pub about the filming. Stan had no recollection that they had filmed the animals at all.

"Oh! You mean those furry things!" he said.

*

When *Out of Town* started sea angling in the shows, they decided to go turbot fishing off a sand bank, just off the coast of France. They stayed at a hotel in Folkestone, over a hundred miles from their homes, where they were told by the skipper of the boat they had hired that it was too rough to go out. They did find a fisherman who was going out, for purely financial reasons. He needed the money and he was due to leave in the middle of the night. Jack and Stan joined him to film the sequence, but the weather was so bad they were sick for the entire journey. The crew laid three miles of long hooked line and then waited. Three hours passed. Jack had been ill for eight, but soon they had caught over £500 worth of turbot. In the midst of it all, Stan had filmed one of the best sequences he had ever made. Neither of them knew how he had done it.

Stan was often accused by Jack of having second sight; he seemed to have an uncanny ability of knowing what was going to happen. When Jack thought a shot was over, Stan would often keep his finger on the button. "When he does," said Jack, "You can guarantee that something will happen." While fishing for roach in the Dorset Stour in the middle of a very good day, Jack told Stan to stop filming. "We've got enough now," he said.

Jack, however, being the eternally optimistic fisherman, pushed the float out one more time, hooking a huge roach. Stan started the camera. Jack wondered why he needed yet another film of a roach on a hook when, just as he was pulling it from the water, an enormous pike rolled over, took the roach and swam away. Of course, Stan had it all in the can.

Another instance of Stan's second sight, when shooting a ferreting film, proved quite amusing. Traditionally, ferreting would take place on Boxing Day afternoon, when the men would take all the children and dogs out, leaving the women to wash up. They decided to make a film out of this traditional Boxing Day pursuit on a rather frosty day with both dogs and grandchildren in tow. They had had quite a good day until they lost a ferret, possibly stuck behind a rabbit down a hole. They would have to dig for it, but first they had to listen for scratches to find approximately where it was. A child was following on, listening at every hole, just like his grandparent. Suddenly the ferret forced the rabbit away and it bolted out of a hole. The child happened to be peering down the very same hole at precisely that moment with the result that both child and rabbit met, nose to nose, each jumping back wildly in the air with everyone falling about laughing.

"My God!" Jack said to Stan, laughing. "I wish we'd got that on film!"

"We have!" he replied, triumphantly.

Sometimes, of course, they just hit lucky. Stan recalls the making of one of his particular favourite films; his recollections are also telling insights into the filming methods employed:

"This was the life cycle of the Grannon Fly, known at that time to exist on only twelve rivers in the world. Lord Radner's estate, just south of Salisbury, was one of them. The river bailiff phoned me at home one day to tell me that the hatch had begun, so I dashed over and got film of the larvae floating up from the river bed and emerging, rather like a mayfly, to float down the river, riding on their casing while their wings dried off. Many were eaten by trout, but survivors floated downstream and eventually flew off into the vegetation on the river bank. There they mated and flew upstream to gain the ground that they had lost on the way down. The females then walked down anything that protruded from the water and, as flies, laid their eggs deep down to start the cycle again. A fortunate rain storm ended the hatch, so I had part of a day to design and build new underwater equipment and I had a second day to complete. Some days later I took inserts of Jack watching what was going on. Some months later I took inserts of Jack and the Country Boy watching what was going on.

When the programme was transmitted, Jack had discovered a new book written by a very eminent specialist who said that he had visited the right rivers at the right time over many years but had never seen a hatch and had therefore concluded that the Grannon Fly story was a myth."

*

Although Stan remained unmoved by much of the material he filmed, he did eventually buy a boat for the purpose of fishing and actually became something of an expert on the flounder.

The director of *Out of Town*, George Egan, had turned up for the first few programmes, but quickly realised that Jack and Stan didn't really need him. Each day's shooting was planned out by the two of them first thing in the morning, then they edited it mentally before deciding to shoot anything which occurred in either late morning or afternoon. They simply talked through the probable shooting requirements in the morning and shot it as light permitted. Sometimes they could make two films in a day, especially when fishing on a stretch of river where Jack could go for different types of fish. Once filming had begun they hardly talked to one another. The scenes were always filmed on positive stock which meant that the film was not a negative. This was then used for the purpose of editing at a later stage. The whole process might take many months after the film was shot, and the soundtrack could be dubbed in the studio as late as the day before it was to be broadcast.

The series usually started around October and finished around March, this being the time for holidays, and from April onwards they would film right through the late spring and summer. Subjects were filmed either at the appropriate or the best time of year to maximise the likelihood of success, with periods of good weather reserved for photography, and in late summer the films were put together for broadcast in the new season.

On top of this came the ideas, letters and requests for Jack to make an *Out of Town* film at various venues, all of which had to be checked for their suitability. They usually completed about a hundred days of filming each year and edited them, for the most part, in the six weeks prior to going on air, ending up with a collection of stories which were then edited into programmes.

Jack was of the firm opinion that the show should be topical. For example, films about shooting should be broadcast when shooting was in season, but all that changed one winter after Isobel had said she was sick of the winter weather and could do with some sunshine. For a change, Jack broadcast a summertime film at Christmas, which proved a great success. From that year on topicality took a back seat.

At first the programmes were only fifteen to twenty minutes long with no break. They dealt with just one subject followed by a 'talk in the shed' designed to complement it. Then Cyril Bennett, a television controller in the capital, decided to try it on the air in London. Cyril thought it was probably of more interest to people in London than it was to country folk who were surrounded by it every day. The London broadcasts were a great success and eventually led to *Out of Town* being shown all over the country. A number of changes to the show's format were needed for this to happen; it would have to become a half hour programme with a commercial break. This gave Jack the opportunity to split the programme into two. There would be an introduction, a link to the second half and then a short feature followed by a longer feature after the break. Jack worried about the break and its likely effect on the continuity of the programme. This was solved by their decision to have two contrasting subjects in each half of the programme.

Around two thirds of the material was of summer activities, leaving the rest for winter pursuits. Black and white film proved perfectly adequate for the original programmes, but as soon as they opted for colour they found they needed twice as much light, which became a problem in the shorter winter days. They suffered very badly from dull days, and the countryside changed so much in terms of light that a wide range of exposures were needed, and different approaches became necessary for filming the same piece of landscape on consecutive days. A river that was as clear as a bell one day would be like pea soup on another, or in flood, or would even dry up. Wild duck flying in large numbers would have taken off and gone by the time they were ready to begin filming them. It wasn't the ideas that held them back, but rather the unpredictable nature of the countryside. Jack said he sometimes wished he was making pop films, where it was pretty well certain that the planned event would occur on cue.

It had been their intention to make a film about swallows and what they did before the days when there were telegraph wires on which they could sit. The swallow did, without doubt, predate the invention of the telegraph wire. Jack had a spine oak in his garden; it was a dead oak tree, probably about two hundred years old, and Jack had always wondered about making a film about the hundreds of swallows that would gather in families in its branches before setting off for Africa. He arranged to shoot it one Thursday with Stan, and happily watched them on the Wednesday evening, excited about the next day's filming. Of course, come the morning, they had all gone, leaving Stan and Jack to wait another twelve months.

Each year began with a notebook containing around a hundred or so ideas which Jack wanted to film. Some of them were never made, even though they were included in the book for five years running. Others turned up without any planning at all. Jack had heard of and met the last remaining elderly lady making the famous Dowton Pillow Lace. It had been made for the Royal trousseau for many generations in the villages along the Hampshire Avon, and the tradition had survived up until the 1950s. In the space of the last ten years, however, the skill had all but vanished. Jack met the very last remaining practitioner and filmed her, all within two days. The notebook invariably took a back seat when unexpected opportunities such as this arose.

One thing they learned quickly about shooting the scenes was to maintain strict secrecy over the subject and location. In the early days of filming, they had been shooting by a trout stream on land owned by a farmer friend of Jack's. The programme went out on a Friday and by the following Monday there were dozens of cars and vans on the land, each a fishing hopeful looking to emulate Jack. The farmer rang him, saying, "I'll never forgive you; there are twenty-eight cars on my land!"

Jack out fishing with Oliver Kite.

One of the few criticisms levelled at the *Out of Town* series was with regard to Jack's dress sense. In an age when many presenters still wore formal dress, Jack had chosen to dress for the part; a morning suit and bow tie would have looked ever so conspicuous in many of the shots. Indeed, the first programme in his earlier *Gone Fishing* series was intended to begin with a reverse striptease as Jack, beginning in his underwear, would don layer after layer until sealed for the purpose. When Oliver Kite, the famous television fisherman and naturalist, died, Jack dedicated an entire programme to him as a fitting obituary. One viewer wrote in the following comment to Jack. "At the time I was shaving and my boy shouted up that Jack Hargreaves was on the television. I asked what he was on about and he replied that it must be something important because he's wearing a tie."

Jack received one of the ultimate accolades available to a television producer in 1978 when two episodes of the *Out of Town* series were chosen for preservation in the National Film Archive so that, "When they finally cover Britain with concrete, they will have something to remind them of what it was all about." The films selected were 'Book Binding', originally broadcast in two parts on January the sixth and January the thirteenth, 1978 and 'Bee Skips', from March the seventeenth the same year.

The Book Binding programme was always a particular favourite of Stan's. He recalls that the film "was shot in a tiny workroom near Fawley - so small that Jack had to go away while I did the filming. My first job was as a junior estimating clerk in a big printing works, so I knew the process well. The film was edited down to cover two weeks' worth of programmes and Jack was reluctant to transmit it. Then he became ill one Christmas and it had to be used, and it got an enormous audience response."

One of the programme's best remembered features remains to this day the point at the end of the programme when Jack would produce an object whose purpose inevitably generated various degrees of puzzlement; indeed, this was the whole point as Jack simply asked the audience if they knew what it was. Ever the showman, Jack often pretended ignorance although in most cases he certainly did know the answer. His purpose was always to generate curiosity and interest in the item and as such he played his own part in bringing it back to life if only for a moment as we discussed it among ourselves. Perhaps he was also the inventor of inter-active television years before the term was to become common in the digital age.

Out of Town came to an end when Southern Television lost its ITV franchise in December 1981, and Jack said his farewell to the Southern Television viewers, saluting them with a glass of dark ale and a heartfelt "Cheerio!" It was, however, not the end of Jack's career as a television advocate for all things rural. After all, he still had a long list of ideas in his notebook!

On the demise of Southern Television, Stan decided to stay on with the new franchised company, Television South (TVS), but Jack teamed up with Lacewing Productions to make further programmes of *Out of Town*, renamed *Old Country*. Lacewing was founded by Dave Knowles, who at Southern Television had been the editor for *Out of Town* and was chosen by Jack to work on the new *Old Country* series. Over the ensuing years, from 1983 to 1985, three *Old Country* series of twenty programmes each, sixty programmes in all, were broadcast by Channel 4.

The filming, editing and post-production of *Old Country* were all done from scratch. Jack had an abundance of fresh ideas and there was no need plagiarise any material that had been produced before. Jack would go out location shooting with Steve Wagstaff, a freelance cameraman who was already working regularly on Lacewing productions. Jack and Steve developed a relationship much akin to the one that Jack had with Stan, starting each day with a plan for the story they were going to tell and then filming intuitively, practically without the need for words. This way of working, as before, allowed a 'story' to develop, and on more than one occasion led to capturing unexpected 'magic moments' that made the programmes so alive.

Jack location filming with Steve Wagstaff (both on cart).

After filming, the 'rushes' (filmed footage) was edited by Dave Knowles, as it had been at Southern Television, and all the sound effects were then dubbed onto the edited film. When each series of stories were ready, a 'studio' was booked for Jack's 'to camera' bits and for the live recording of his commentary over the already edited stories. The *Old Country* studio was Meonstoke village hall, where Jack's original shed set from Southern Television days was set up on the stage and a crew for lighting, sound recording and camera attended … to all effects it was just as it had been in the Southern Television studio. A fuller description of the making of *Old Country* can be found at the end of this book.

Channel 4 launched in November 1982 and for the first time Jack realised his ambition to achieve the full networking of his programme, meaning that it was available to people all over the country. *Out of Town* had been broadcast by Southern Television, but it had never been fully networked.

After three series, Channel 4 decided to call it a day; they had a total of sixty films with freedom to use them whenever they wished. Jack, now aged seventy-five, accepted it as some form of retirement from broadcast media. Thus, the programme, itself so often copied and having remained fundamentally the same since its birth in 1960, came to an end.

On the loss of the franchise by Southern Television, Jack had been given, in lieu of a pension, the rights to the *Out of Town* library. Not one to let a good idea die, Jack wanted to do something with this material, and in 1986 he agreed with Primetime to make a package of re-edited and re-presented programmes from the *Out of Town* programme material. So it was that Jack and some members of the original *Old Country* crew used material from the old programmes to make a series of DVDs, which are still available.

Jack in his shed with the *Out of Town* archive.

Chapter 7
The Boardroom Broadcaster

Although the *Out of Town* series ran for some twenty two years, it was not an immediate national success. The regional television companies were very different from the major corporate organisation we know today and schedules would have been unrecognisable to anyone travelling to the other side of the country and tuning in to ITV. The networks were independent companies and drew up their own schedules which comprised of regional programmes with just perhaps one or two making it to all networks, but even these would be broadcast at different times or different days according to which network you were tuned in to. It might even be months or a year until a programme seen in one locality made it to another.

Such was the case with *Out of Town*. Initially it was broadcast only in the Southern Television region, until it was picked up by broadcasters in London. It was not until 1968 that the programme became truly national, with Jack Hargreaves having already become something of a national celebrity through other appearances. In truth this is only partially representative of Jack's activities, much of which actually occurred behind the scenes making programmes happen rather than making them himself.

His curriculum vitae for the period is quite fascinating and suggests something of a restless nature and an irrepressible energy. During his time at Southern Television he continued with other projects of interest to him. He also joined Associated Rediffusion as an Executive Producer, where he stayed until 1965, by coincidence, the year he ended his association with Hobson Bates to both his and Isobel's relief. She didn't like the boardroom and she was too busy with Jack's other work to put up with the inconvenience Hobson Bates was throwing her way. While Jack had been in America, she had written to him saying she was looking forward to the day she could leave. They had by then formed a company called Out of Town Ltd. to run the making of the films and this took up the majority of her time. Jack had long finished the reorganisation at Hobson Bates' creative department and had no real desire to throw himself back into the world of advertising copy.

During the early years of the swinging sixties he appeared in a number of radio quiz shows including *Round Britain Quiz* with his old friend Roy Plomley. He was also a regular on television in a quiz programme called *Dad, you're a Square*.

In addition to working in front of the cameras, Jack joined Southern Television as an Executive Producer, rising rather quickly to the position of Deputy Controller of Programmes. Once again he was in his element, under pressure and working hard. He was directly responsible for a number of programmes, as well as being charged with developing children's television. He served on the Children's Television Committee of the Independent Broadcasting Authority (IBA) for many years and had a huge influence in developing output, overseeing the development of many children's programmes now viewed as both groundbreaking and world class.

From 1959, Southern Television had been producing children's programmes, none of which had been seen outside their own region. These included *Animal ABC* and *Model World*, some of which Jack presented himself. He was also involved in the production of a reportage programme for teenagers called *Three Go Round* which involved a young Fred Dinenage.

Following Jack's participation in programming for Southern Television, every one of their children's programmes came to be sold around the country. Jack became responsible for some sixty programmes a year, many of them highly memorable for both the viewer and the industry as a whole; *Danger Island*, *The New Forest Rustlers* and *Freewheelers* were among his drama output, and his comedies included *Bright's Boffins*. These successful shows encouraged the company's ambition, culminating in a production of Robert Louis Stevenson's *Black Arrow*, a series whose costume bill alone would have been unthinkable just a few years earlier.

The backbone of the children's information series was *How*, a programme Jack had conceived in the form of *Know How* in 1964. Its origin was a distant memory of Jack's from his school years as an eccentric teacher had brought an open umbrella into the classroom to illustrate a lesson about the earth's axis. He had discussed the idea with Angus Wright, a producer at Southern who himself recalled a similar experience in a classroom. He had then taken it to Cyril Bennett and John Rhodes, both senior executives at Southern Television. It embodied

Jack's conviction that interest was as important to children as the mere notion of entertainment. He envisaged a programme made with a sense of fun but addressing the young audience as equals. He also wanted presenters who were "not always damn well smiling."

His first recruit for the project was the young Fred Dinenage. Jack's rather unusual interview technique involved inviting Fred on a trip down the Canal du Midi in France, an opportunity he jumped at having never been outside the United Kingdom. He soon realised, however, that his role was to drive Stan Bréhaut's van while Jack, Isobel and Stan would sail off for the day. Fred would simply drive the van to a prearranged point where they would all stay the night. Astutely, Jack spent the time observing Fred to learn what kind of person he was. He believed a presenter did his job of communicating not only with words, but also with his personality, and the week and a half they spent together would hopefully confirm his suitability for the role.

The show was to be a studio based programme which would run as a series of individual items running as alternate long and short pieces. The long items would be filmed prior to the broadcast, but the short items would go out live. Each piece would attempt to explain and answer a question which would always begin with 'How do they ...?' An example of which might be 'How do they catch smugglers?' with the answer being an explanation of the role of Customs and Excise or 'How do they bring a large ship into Southampton?' which would entail explaining the role of the Harbour Master.

Fred Dinenage recalls that the initial pilot for the series was aimed at adults and was screened late at night. It was well received but a little boring and needed a considerable rethink with regard to detail. With its eventual emphasis on Native Americans and a memorable theme tune, it became the perfect vehicle for Jack's original idea. By this time, he had acquired a position of considerable power at Southern Television and if he thought something to be a good idea there were few who would argue otherwise in any case, so the details were tweaked and *How* came into existence. It was first broadcast in 1966.

In addition to Fred and Jack, the other two presenters were Bunty James and Jon Miller. Bunty was a great provider of ideas for the show including numerous items on cookery. Her most famous contribution was 'How to make a doll's house from an envelope.' She was eventually replaced by Marian Davies. Jon Miller was always the serious member of the team and was thought of as the 'machine man'. He was actually a marine biologist with an insatiable thirst for scientific knowledge. His experiments were not always guaranteed to go well, but the general view was that if they messed up it was great television! Explaining why it had gone wrong would always beat lecturing on how it worked.

Jon Miller's best remembered piece was demonstrating his own invention; the 'Cheerer Upper.' It was designed to compliment you on your appearance and then to offer you a cup of tea. During a live show it emptied the contents of the cup into his lap!

Fred Dinenage was seen as the 'action man' of the team. If anyone was to be shot out of an aeroplane in an ejector seat or to loop the loop in a glider it was Fred. His worst memory was of flying upside down in an open cockpit aeroplane in which he was not properly strapped into position. He remembers his early years on the programme as a time when he continually got things wrong. He recalls, "There was water everywhere, things breaking and me messing up generally all the time." He felt sure he would be kicked off the team if he didn't improve so, in an attempt to save his floundering career, he took to studying in detail each subject he was to present and worked overtime with his props.

Following a number of programmes where everything had gone well, he felt that his future was secure, but he was taken aside by Jack. "You're getting it all wrong," he said in a very serious tone. Fred argued that nothing was going wrong. If anything, it was all working perfectly well now, only to be shot down by the comment, "The truth is you were employed to be the prat of the group!"

From that time on Fred never looked back. "I built my career on being a prat, and it has worked ever since!" he comments, looking back fondly on those days spent working with the team. The combination of Jack's razor sharp mind and his keen sense of fun leave memories of a man he looked up to and admired greatly. He also remembers, with a smile, an incident which happened on more than one occasion on air. Jack was the only one ever allowed to smoke on the set; he said his pipe was actually a prop and as such the audience expected to see him smoking it even though he didn't necessarily want to smoke it. He would fill three pipes and smoke one of them. As he finished one he would put it in his pocket and light another. "The problem was," said Fred, "that sometimes the pipe wasn't actually out." Fred recalls a set hand occasionally having to crawl along the floor with a glass of water and pouring it into Jack's pocket to put the fire out. Ever the professional Jack would just continue his piece to camera without even flinching.

The iconic photo of Jack which he sent out to his fans.

How ran through nine series in total and is, in effect, still in existence to this day. The format has changed somewhat and the show now has a slightly more energetic presentation. It is now also called *How 2* but in essence it is much the same. By coincidence, even this more frenetic approach to informative programmes for children can be traced back to the innovative imagination of Jack Hargreaves who, after the final series of *How* was responsible for *Run-Around* with Mike Reid, numerous guests, many of them pop stars, and lots of running children.

*

Fred also recalls the way that many big name producers from London would appear at Southern Television to see Jack. Their immediate thought was to the effect that he was some kind of country bumpkin. He did not wear the right clothes, he certainly did not look like a television executive, he often sported several days' stubble and he blew clouds of pipe smoke in their faces. This, combined with his old-world politeness and etiquette, gave him the air of a wartime boffin. As a result, they almost always underestimated him and he would have them eating out of his hand within a short time.

Although *How* and the earliest incarnations of *Out of Town* are undoubtably the best remembered of Jack's output from this period, they were only two of many ideas and inventions which sprang from his fertile and imaginative mind. As an extension of his successful formula from *How* he proposed 'How did they?' an historical version, and even an etiquette programme called 'How to be ladies and gentlemen?' He also proposed 'How did you?' intended as a series of brief interviews with celebrities and adventurers.

Prior to his work developing *How*, Jack had spent time in America and had produced a series of documentaries for the US market called *On the Edge of Abundance*. He became fascinated with the role of America and the lead it was giving to the rest of the world. In the 1960s the spending power of the average American citizen was some 70% greater than their British counterpart and in just nine days that same average American would spend the same as the average Indian would spend in an entire year. The economics were undeniably impressive, but they failed to excite Jack; his fascination lay in the effect of these facts on the individual. He also knew that whatever happened in the US would inevitably influence events in the UK and he was concerned by both the prospect of change and the speed with which it seemed to take place. What he realised then is only now beginning to gain ground with the environmental lobby; technology alone is not the main thrust of our environmental problems, but human culture, which develops as we embrace it, and which will determine how these changes affect us as both individuals and as a society.

He brought the concept back to the UK with the intention of running it as *Big City Blues*, a series of half hour programmes, each focussing on one of a series of overlapping ideas, but with a central theme examining the stresses placed on people by urbanisation and mechanisation. It was broadcast as *Big Town Britain* by Associated Rediffusion in 1964, with Jack writing the following as the introductory notes for the series:

> "Man has certain biological needs and capabilities which are largely unaltered - and unalterable - since the time they served as essential equipment for primitive human life. As his environment has developed technically, and in density and in pace and many other ways, man has tried to adapt by following in turn a succession of

philosophical and ethical and religious concepts outside of himself. Each of these has in turn become conventionalised and has lingered on after it has failed to serve."

Jack's time in America had also made him aware that many of the young people who would eventually hold positions of power and influence would do so not because their parents had done so, but as a result of their own abilities. Our own society, too, was becoming a meritocracy; perhaps Jack himself was an early example of the trend. He felt that we needed to know a little about these people in their formative years and interviewed them himself in a series of programmes called *Young Tigers*, also broadcast in 1964.

Among those interviewed were Mary Quant the fashion designer, Colin Davies the conductor, and Peter Hall the theatre director. Jack demonstrated a no-nonsense approach to interviewing. As he put it his role was "getting their skin off" and he did this by the most minimalist of techniques, drawing on the influence of John Freeman in his influential *Face to Face* series. The critics were very enthusiastic. The Sunday Times described his technique as "masterful, able to keep his mouth shut yet able to bring out the very best of his subjects." Sadly, in spite of this high praise, only six programmes were ever made.

In fact, much of Jack's concern about the human condition centred on its reaction to change. He produced a programme called *Suppressed Violence* in which he explored Bertrand Russell's view that is was dangerous to abolish war without providing an appropriate substitute. In it he tried to answer the question 'How can we use the violence that is natural to the male in a mechanised society?' He then explored the changing role of women in a programme titled *Sexless Society* in which his concerns centred on the new type of career woman who was no longer prepared to follow the example set by her mother.

In a broadcast called *Artistic Leisure* he challenged the notion of the arts as the exclusive preserve of the academically educated members of society, citing among other the Salford painter Lowry and the renowned colliery brass bands of Yorkshire to illustrate his point that the arts were simply a product of man's need for self-expression, and culture was merely a means of making life bearable irrespective of our station in life.

One programme, which sadly never saw the light of day, was *Never a Whole Job to Do* in which Jack set out to examine the disappearance of the artisan class. He had intended to examine the fact that modern production techniques reduce us to a small part of the creative process, unlike our forebears who could stand back and admire the 'art' of what they themselves had produced. It had echoes of Charlie Chaplin's dilemmas in *Modern Times* as he struggled to combat the dehumanising effect of production line manufacturing.

Jack was proud of these programmes and viewed them as his contribution to the world of adult television. They marked him out as a serious broadcaster. Although no one was ever in any real doubt as to his credentials it did concern him that he was becoming somewhat stereotyped as either a representative of the quaint world of the countryside or the sometimes flippant world of children's television. Ironically, as Jack must have been aware, there were, after a couple of years, as many adult viewers tuning in to *How* as there were children. Wherever the four members of the team travelled, they were likely to be accosted by both young and old with right hand raised and the familiar deep voiced 'How' followed by a beaming smile.

To give Jack credit, his role on the Children's Broadcast Committee on behalf of Southern Television did raise the profile of children's programmes and indeed their quality. He made children's broadcasting 'adult' in that he raised its profile, made sure it had sufficient funding and worked to the maxim that, as it was for children it had damn well be better than any corresponding adult programme. As Jack said, "It is not because children are less imaginative than adults; they are just more critical."

Jack's other rural series, which generally raises a smile as people recall it, is the series *Country Boy*, a pure piece of nostalgia which reflected many of his experiences not just with Simon Baddeley, his stepson, but also when he was the apprentice himself with Victor Pargeter. It was a fond memory of their hunting and shooting together, their strolls through the country, their cart rides, their fishing and their sailing.

The series began with Dennis Goulding, and later Mike Borne, in the role of the boy from the town and his education in country ways. Jack had understood well before the advent of the Countryside Alliance that a culture gap had separated the country and the city. It was a beautifully understated programme and, in the case of Mike Borne, it did actually involve his spending two weeks at a time in the company of both Jack and Isobel where their time together was filmed by Stan Bréhaut. He was to stay with them many times after the series had ended and indeed returned the kindness by inviting them up to Fulham.

Jack on location with a 'countryman' and Country Boy, Mike Borne.
This photograph is a fine example of Stan Bréhaut's work, which could not be appreciated fully from the poor television pictures of the time.

To Jack, *Country Boy* was more important in many ways than *Out of Town* because it gave him the opportunity to explain to a wider audience something of the misunderstanding which clouded the relationship between town and country. In all three series were made, but it was then dropped for a number of reasons, some technical but also a third series would have required a third boy as Mike was beginning to grow up.

Jack, Mike Borne and Isobel.

One further programme remembered by many but rarely associated with Jack was the long-running series *House Party*. The show began in the 1960's and ran until the late 1970's. It was a general interest show for women and consisted of a large kitchen table sited in a country style kitchen. A number of women would sit around and discuss various topics of interest. It is a format that has been copied many times since. Jack was in overall control of the show and his friend Steve Wade, Head of Outside Broadcasting, directed the show from time to time. Steve's wife was actually interviewed for a position on the show, but Jack prevented her joining. "We don't have wives working for us!"

*

Jack was able to cash in considerably on his television success. It had exposed him to a large number of ordinary people who effectively invited him into their lounges each week. As he was also viewed by them as an expert on a range of subjects, his name and face were sought after to sell things, in particular items associated with the country. His management agent, Bagenal Harvey, organised for him to be photographed by Great Universal Stores for Kay's Catalogue. He sold fishing gear and clothes. It was certainly quite profitable, netting him £118.2s.6d. every two months in 1964, no small amount when you consider that this was the cost of a small family car at the time. He also marketed fishing and shooting equipment and produced a series of Christmas cards which were sold all over the world.

Jack was never more at home than in his country clothes.

Chapter 8
High Expectations

It is evident that *Out of Town* changed Jack's life in many ways. It certainly gave him real financial security through both the programme's popularity and the fame and credibility it brought him. As such he was never afraid to sell himself or use this popularity to further a particular end or desire. One such desire took shape in a plan he formulated in the early 1970's when he had drawn up a document proposing an expansion of the Out of Town (Lymington) limited company he had set up with Isobel. It involved the creation of an Out of Town Centre.

At the time the notion was quite novel. Only safari parks and zoos were then offering people an escape to a more countrified attraction, although they really had very little to do with our own rural heritage. Indeed, Jack proposed the setting up of a larger number of centres with the intention of offering people a chance to take part in country sports and pursuits, reflecting much of the content of the television programme he had successfully developed.

Jack was realistic in appraising the company's likely main resource. 'The Company has one unique asset, namely Mr. Jack Hargreaves,' he wrote, aware that he would be able to sell the title *Out of Town* to potential investors as a self-publicising product as long as it continued to be broadcast. Potential for sales, however, lay not only in entrance fees, but also in the provision of training, facilities, equipment and merchandise. Jack had even set out the basic requirements in terms of property together with plans to convert it into a working centre.

Unfortunately, nothing came of the original proposals, and they lay dormant for several years, eventually resurfacing as a proposal for a charitable trust with an altogether more philanthropic aim. His vision involved city children being given an introduction to the country by both living in and taking part in a mixed husbandry enterprise. They would milk cows and take part in a wide range of what might be referred to as 'chores' on the average smallholding.

Jack's search for an appropriate site led him to Beaulieu. He already enjoyed a friendship with Lord Montagu as he had been a member of the Beaulieu shoot for over twenty years. He was also aware that Home

Farm, the estate's own working farm and original provider of food for the estate, would shortly be available to rent. The two men certainly knew each other well enough to discuss aspects of finance regarding the centre and indeed did so in 1975, the idea taking shape in Jack's mind as a project which might fill his retirement years.

Home Farm seemed to present the ideal opportunity. It was a beautiful site surrounded by woods which sloped gently down to the Beaulieu River. It covered some fifty acres and was separated into various fields ranging in size from two to twelve acres. Each field was fully watered, but it appears the fencing needed major work. It had a river which was tidal and was available for river trips down into the estuary and the Solent as well as along the nature reserves which lined its own banks. There were, in addition, several cottages, a Dutch barn, piggeries, deep litter houses and various implement sheds.

*

By coincidence, at the same time Jack was contemplating the Out of Town Centre, Lord Montagu was looking to improve public use of his own facilities by setting up the Countryside Educational Trust. Jack would have needed his own charitable trust to get his venture of the ground and, to save time, he agreed, instead, to become a founder trustee of Lord Montagu's Countryside Educational Trust. He did, however, make clear his wish that the Trust and the Out of Town Centre be considered as wholly separate ventures with their own finances and management. His motives for this are uncertain. He may have wanted future freedom to commercialise the project, or he may simply have mistrusted the management at the Beaulieu Estate. As regards control of the project, Jack was convinced that his exclusive and innate understanding of the countryside placed him in a unique position to determine how it should be communicated. Perhaps he felt that the job of doing this was too important to be trusted to others.

Unlike the earlier project which had been designed as a means of inspiring investors to provide funding, the new project would require a large investment from Jack himself in terms of both time and effort. As with the earlier proposal, the name Jack Hargreaves would carry considerable weight in seeking funds. Initial estimates for the venture were high and ran to approximately £200,000 to set up the place, and £46,000 per year to run it. It was believed that half of this could be found from the children attending the centre, but Jack also wanted to erect a series of buildings to serve as dormitories, teaching rooms, recreational space and dining rooms. The time needed to get the project up to its full working capacity would be three years.

Jack envisaged finance and support for the centre coming from just a small number of powerful individuals and groups but found that hundreds of *Out of Town* viewers and numerous fishing clubs and agricultural and sports societies were keen to donate. Jack himself approached everyone he could think of to get the project off the ground and found that the Director General of the IBA, the NFU, the Chairman of the British Deer Society, the Surveyor of the New Forest, senior officials at Hampshire County Council and many local landowners, among others, were all supportive of the project. This further encouraged Jack, who felt he could promote both the ideals and the finance for the project by simply talking to people, as he put it, "even if it takes a hundred lunches and fifty after dinner speeches."

Jack saw the centre being run as a subsistence farm adapted to teaching and run by a small initial staff which would include a farmer and his wife with clerical support being bought in from the Beaulieu Estate. It was Jack's "unashamed dream that one day there will be many Centres in different places, all run by *Out of Town* governors." To achieve this vision Jack wanted control of the project and it was in his inability to maintain that control that he began to see his dream slipping away.

A surprise decision by the Inner London Education Authority (ILEA) to donate a large sum of money came in the spring of 1976. The sum was apparently sourced from a fund which they found difficult to allocate due to the social criteria set by the government. Southern Television then promised to match the funding from ILEA, both bodies pledging seventy thousand pounds which would enable the project to get off the ground straight away. It would be hard to imagine that this level would come without strings and in this case the price was to be Jack's effective control of the centre's education policy.

Perhaps naively, Jack had seen the centre as a way of inspiring children in the same way that he himself had been inspired by Victor Pargeter as a child. Modern education was, however, very different; it was ruled by learning objectives, targets and health and safety regulations and, along with their money, the ILEA brought a need for their own controls and modern educational thought. More to the point, they also brought a parochial attitude to the project. In their eyes the centre was 'purchased' for the use of 'their' children and there was little desire to share it with pupils from other education authorities, even those from the region covered by Southern Television which had generously matched the ILEA donation pound for pound. Jack himself was of the view that the directors at Southern Television were rather less than forceful in the matter than they might have been. He began to feel vulnerable as a battle commenced for possession of the centre.

'I find myself unhappy about the Out of Town Centre,' he wrote at the head of a five page aide-memoir. He was convinced that he had made two serious mistakes. The first had been to join with Lord Montagu's Countryside Education Trust. He had initially been swayed by the positive feedback he had received, but in reality the trust had had very little money. He felt, with hindsight, that they had simply seen an opportunity to gain from an association with television in the promotion of the centre, but as Jack had been prepared to use the same connection in securing funding he was perhaps being rather naïve. The second mistake he considered to be taking public funding too early before the Out of Town Centre had established its own reputation which might then have been used as a convincing argument for Jack's own idea of how the centre should be run. As it was he saw the project moving towards a series of educational 'bite size chunks' rather than his own vision of an overall sense of what the countryside was about. He was also unhappy when informed that teachers would have a say in how actual lessons would take place. He felt they would know little more than the children themselves and feared the whole project becoming "farm walks with clipboards and information packs, rather than a root experience."

One of the directors of Lord Montagu's Countryside Educational Trust was a Mr. Carter who had been a head teacher. He was viewed as the ideal candidate to direct the Out of Town Centre. It could be argued that his understanding of both the methods and culture of current educational thinking would have served well within the trust's aim of informing children, but the very idea sent Jack into a fury. He rejected Mr. Carter's candidacy and, as a consequence, he found himself in permanent disagreement with his partners in the project.

Jack felt under considerable pressure and he considered that he should leave the project behind but was not prepared to go without a fight. He took the step of contacting all the regional education authorities within the Southern Television region. He felt that their support might enable him to regain the control he was losing fast. He was, however, thwarted by ILEA who had already spoken to the relevant education authorities and were already armed with their agreement that all educational methods at the centre must be determined according to current guidelines.

Jack no longer saw his aim as viable. He wrote, 'I am sure I have been naive, but I am disillusioned and the matter has now become an anxiety from which I cannot escape ... In what had developed I can recognise nothing of what I originally visualised.' This contrasted with an earlier minute of the Trust which had stated:

'Mr. Hargreaves outlined the objectives of the Out of Town project, namely to obtain a lease on Home Farm which was currently held on a grazing licence and to develop it as a small mixed farm. There would be simple residential accommodation to allow children aged 8-12 years to spend a week or two at Home Farm in order to become thoroughly familiar with the countryside.'

The Out of Town Centre did get off the ground and provides a wonderful experience for many children. It is perhaps now something more of a heritage centre, although the concept of such was not around in the mid 1970's. An early publicity leaflet described a modern facility for thirty children and their teachers; very much the project as it still is today. The leaflet stated, 'The Out of Town Centre has been founded by Southern Television and the Inner London Education Authority with the support of the Beaulieu Estate.' It did not mention Jack Hargreaves, except as a name in the list of governors.

Jack's interest in the Out of Town Centre did enable him to see it built and functioning. It is still going strong, having recently enjoyed many consecutive bumper years. Its staff are enthusiastic and children do undeniably gain a little hands-on experience of the very thing which Jack sought to pass on. He himself never taught at the centre and his involvement did not become the retirement project he had envisaged, but his original plan had been hatched on his own experiences just after the First World War and times had changed. You could not take on thirty children unused to the fields and meadows in the same way that one sympathetic farmer had taken one rebellious youth some sixty years earlier and opened his eyes to a new world.

In the 1980s Jack stood down from his position on the board of the Countryside Educational Trust. Although he had not seen his vision realised, his inspiration had shone through, bringing benefits to many thousands of children over several decades. Today it is understandable that modern educators would insist on using modern educational methods to impart knowledge, especially when their own budgets had gone into funding the project. Equally, you would expect that a man of Jack Hargreaves's experience would wish to do things his way. This had not been a battle between heroes and villains, but rather one of differing good intentions where no real common ground could exist. Reading through reams of paper from Jack's files, he viewed the problems with the Out of Town Centre as very much symptomatic of the misunderstanding between town and country. It was somewhat ironic that one of his greatest disappointments had its roots so deeply entwined in the very clash of cultures he sought to explain to an increasingly urban population, much of which had rural aspirations.

Chapter 9
Ask the Experts

Of course, it was Jack's abilities as a communicator which earned him respect, but as with all great communicators it was his chosen subject with which the viewer constantly identified him. Consequently, he became labelled with the dubious term 'expert'. He himself professed he was "certainly not an expert except, perhaps, in one thing: a general knowledge of the countryside." We tend to think that a general knowledge is not a comprehensive knowledge, but Jack's meaning was different. If you were brought up in the country there were only country things to occupy you and, as such, they were the things you did.

However short Jack's exposure to the country might have been in his early years, he had been a quick learner; a bored youth with an enquiring mind fuelled by a life so different to that he had known. The Pargeter way of life had become his own adopted life and he absorbed it with vigour, whether ferreting for rabbits, shooting pigeons or following hounds on a pony, all dependent on the seasons which ruled both the harshness of the climate and the routine of the farm. Each year would be a repeat performance, yet entirely different from its predecessor.

Daily routines involved feeding chickens, tending cows and sheep, cutting hay, chopping wood, fetching water, sewing crops and muck-spreading, among other things. For sport they would fish for trout when the spring came, then for chub in summer and for pike in the autumn. They were surrounded by birds and wild plants, and accordingly they came to know how the countryside behaved and lived even down to its smallest constituent part. That did not mean knowing the Latin name for the creature that had landed on your lapel or the bird making the shrill noise in the foliage. That was left for the scientists and Jack never professed to being one of those, although his time spent studying veterinary science might have given him an edge even here.

Of course, given Jack's long periods of exile from the countryside, much of his research came from the literature that dealt with it. This became his tonic during time spent studying to be a vet, when writing and broadcasting, when writing copy and even when taking part in the fight against Adolf Hitler. As a result of this intensive study, he built up a body of knowledge beyond even that common in the farming community.

Ironically, had he depended solely on his farming interests for his living, he would probably have found the level of knowledge he attained denied to him.

It is also true to say that the extensive knowledge Jack acquired was denied to many in times past. For example, he did not see a fish caught with a dry fly until he moved to the south; it was simply a practice which did not happen in the area in which he lived. Today, however, people would not think twice before hopping into the car to fish all over the country and consequently use fly, float and sea hook. Many of them will live in the city. The invention of free time combined with a newfound mobility has led to experts on subjects such as fishing whose base may be the smallest flat in Kilburn, a world away from their chosen field of study. In the modern age of the internet this is even more so.

Jack believed in preservation of the countryside on a wide scale.

Jack was one of these experts. He lived in London for much of his life but fished the chalk streams of the south until he finally moved to a country retreat himself. But his insights did go deep and best of all was his ability to communicate his message.

He wrote:

> 'There are many bird watchers from Hampstead who know more about birds than I do, but they don't know the name of the plant they are standing on when they are looking at the bird.
>
> There are fly fishermen far more expert than I, but, for example,

one of them, one of the greatest fly fishermen in the country said to me one day "Jack, what's that extraordinary bird?" It was a coot, one of the commonest birds on the river.'

Jack said he could never be sufficient of an expert to compete with those around. There were many better horse people who had never caught a fish, many a better shot who knew nothing of horses and many suburban gardeners whose knowledge of growing the most wonderful beetroot exceeded even that of Jack but had scant understanding of how you might catch a mole. Even experts in dressage, perhaps the highest form of riding skill, often had no idea of how you might put a pony into a trap.

Jack did love to meet the experts and viewed the *Out of Town* vehicle as an opportunity to impart their knowledge the wider population, but he also viewed it as a means for the experts themselves to familiarise themselves with the wider field in which their activity took place. He thought this general view to be extremely important if the true value of the countryside was to be preserved. He summed up his position as follows, "A trout fisherman might fight like hell to protect a certain stream where he fished but wouldn't worry too much about a meadow where a particular orchid grows. The view of the country in its totality is such an important one for preservation on a wide scale."

For Jack, meeting the experts was a humbling experience and, like Isaac Newton, he knew what it was like to "stand on the shoulders of giants." He loved to meet like-minded people and did not feel threatened by their expertise; indeed, he learned a great deal from them, absorbing the tips they offered and furthering his own knowledge, but in all circumstances giving credit to the original source if he ever imparted their particular piece of wisdom himself. He became known as a name dropper in some circles, a great irony when you consider that the people whose names he was accused of dropping were probably telling people gleefully of their encounter with him.

Jack gave the following portrait of some of the people he called experts. He reflected that when he opened his mouth on the television, the words which came out depended completely on who had put them there in the first place. He had simply been grateful for the opportunity to learn.

Richard Walker

Jack considered himself a good fisherman until he met Richard Walker. He was an engineer by trade and had applied his astute engineer's mind to fishing in many new and innovative ways. He had held the record for a carp at 44 lbs, a fish which was to live out its remaining thirty years at London Zoo.

Jack went fishing for pike on a lake he didn't know and so, in place of a guide, he took Richard. On the first day Jack was not allowed to fish at all. At Richard's request he rowed up and down the lake all day while his mentor measured the depth of the water with a plumb line. In the pub that evening he constructed a perfect chart of the lake and worked out how they would go about fishing it early next morning. The next day they did indeed catch several large pike from different parts of the lake.

His skills in reading the water became legendary. On Jack's stretch of the River Kennett there were no Barbell. These fish did exist in a pool higher upstream, but not on Jack's familiar patch. When the local water authority cleared some gravel in the pool, Jack thought the Barbell might have moved downstream. He invited Richard who spent the morning and an hour after lunch walking up and down the stretch.

"I'm not sure if the Barbell are here, but if they are, they will be lying just over there," he said. With that he took his rods and within ten minutes he had caught one weighing in at eight pounds. Jack was of the view that it took a real fisherman to catch fish in such a way on unknown waters. He felt that Richard had a huge effect on the fishing public and said, "Walker is the man who could go anywhere and put on a great performance with any fish."

Whenever he fished with Richard, he would make sure to arrive first and then settle down to fish. Richard's arrival sometime later would be accompanied by his booming out, "Good Lord, you'd have thought that a man who'd been fishing for fifty years would have known the first thing about it!" Jack would respond with, "Good morning, Richard," without looking around.

While fishing Richard would sing arias from Italian operas loudly and passionately. Jack even went as far as saying he could be bombastic and aggressive, but he was also on record as describing him as "a great human being". He knew from experience that if anyone had a problem Richard would just get on with sorting it out with a minimum of fuss.

"No need to mention it, old dear," he would say as he was thanked for his intervention.

Stan Stanbury

Stan Stanbury was the clay pigeon champion of Great Britain for thirteen years from the end of the war well into the 1950s. He was one of the best teachers of shooting Jack had known. On the first occasion Jack had met him he had walked into his office at the London Shooting School and had been surprised to find Lord Mountbatten standing there in his underpants, Stan had been training him, but he was overdue for a meeting at the Admiralty. A car had been dispatched with his uniform and Stan's office had doubled as a changing room.

At the time Jack was working on the gentlemen's magazine, *Lilliput*, in partnership with his friend Colin Willock, himself destined for future success with the long running television programme, *Survival*. A photograph had landed on Jack's desk showing five broken clay pigeons, all apparently shot in the air at once. It was an advert for a certain company's shotgun cartridges and their automatic shotguns, with the shot having apparently been made by an American. Jack bet that an Englishmen could do the same, if not better, and he believed that Stan was just the man to prove it.

Jack borrowed a type of repeating shotgun popular in the United States. It was capable of firing more than the standard two shots of a double-barrelled shotgun; without this the attempt would have been guaranteed to fail.

Stan agreed to take up the challenge and they set up five clays in five traps. Stan broke all five, but the photographer failed to catch it on film. In the end it took thirty-two attempts to get the shot right, but on each occasion, Stan had broken all five. He wanted to go one further and attempt the feat with real wood pigeons, which they all viewed as an impossible task. After three weeks of trying, he phoned Jack. "I've found the secret!" he cried. "You have to get a very high one first and let it fall to the ground while you aim at the others."

Stan, the son of a West Country gun shop owner, was a great charmer. When teaching the nobility to shoot he would keep "calling them Sir until they were shooting well, and then afterward he would call them 'M'dear', which was common parlance in Stan's home town."

Sanders Watney

Sanders Watney, Chief Executive of Watney Breweries, would travel to work each day driving a four in hand coach from his house in London. Upon his arrival at the office he would hand over his horses to a driver who would take them back, returning in the evening to pick him up. Jack had met him while handling the brewery's account during his time with Hobson Bates.

He was the inspiration behind the revival of harness driving in England and was regularly asked questions on driving by Jack, both for the *Out of Town* programme and for his own personal interest. Jack had many carriages, several carts, a few small traps, and once even built a Surrey with a fringe on top as featured in *Oklahoma*. Jack was obsessive about both his ponies and his equipage. Even in his final years he spent much time painting and repairing them and even manufacturing various pieces for them.

Sanders Watney was instrumental in the formation of the British Driving Society (BDS) in 1957. Its aim was to encourage and assist those interested in the driving of equine animals. The BDS runs the Sanders Watney Trust which assists disabled people to take part in the driving of horses, ponies and donkeys.

Jennie Loriston-Clarke

Jennie was one of the UK's most illustrious dressage horsewomen. She trained both her own horses and her own grooms. The latter generally became much sought after internationally once they had 'passed out' of her employment. She was a true expert in giving signals to the horse in order to make it do as required, which she described as a fine art. Her stud at Brockenhurst remained home to her very first pony for over thirty years.

Jennie was frequently asked to take horses into the studio, especially for the television *How*. On one occasion her horse froze with fright as it entered into the large studio crammed with specialist lighting, cameras and a very shiny floor. Jennie quietly talked to the animal for a while then pressed it gently forward. The horse's confidence in its rider was such that it felt safe to continue in spite of the thoroughly alien environment.

John Holmes

John started working with sheep dogs in the 1960s and competed in his homeland of Scotland. He met his wife Mary in competition and together they trained dogs professionally. They provided dogs for films, broadcasts and productions such as *The Hound of the Baskervilles* and *The Rats of Hamlyn*.

Jack believed that John's book *Training the Family Dog* was far and away the best ever written on the subject. Jack used his expertise on many occasions, from advising the viewer on selecting a puppy, right through to individual aspects of the training programme. In order to present the subject in as much detail as possible, John bred puppies specifically for the purpose by crossing a bearded collie with a springer spaniel. One of these puppies called 'Ben' was trained to perform comfortably in front of lights and cameras. Jack considered him to be the first canine superstar in the UK who had been bred for the purpose. He enjoyed a long career in television commercials and helped to sell a wide variety of products, from dog food to credit cards. Throughout his long and contented life Ben remained blissfully unaware of his fame.

Jack and John were to do many programmes together and made one which examined the relationship between dogs and people, pointing out the problems which have arisen as a result of dogs now living in crowded human societies. A couple of dogs were trained to illustrate how perfectly well behaved pets can go wild in the country and chase sheep with potentially disastrous consequences. Their training was so precise and complete that the dogs were able to chase sheep right up to the point prior to attacking, at which point a single call was sufficient to bring them off, leaving the animal unharmed.

*

Of course, there were many others who helped Jack regularly with their knowledge and expertise, people like Len Smith, a Gypsy who regularly supported Jack's endeavours over many years. Jack would turn up at Len's home to request help with films on many diverse subjects with the two of them planning the endeavour of the back of an empty cigarette packet or an envelope in his workshop in the New Forest. Len, who sent a well meant 'Kushti bok' (Romany for good luck) to Jack and Isobel each Christmas, was a great pal. He was trusted with the task of repairing the wheels from Jack's carriages and took part in many filming projects. He is now actively involved in Gypsy politics.

Len Smith driving one of Jack's carts.

So, although the perceived wisdom would be to describe Jack as an expert on country matters, the amount of time he spent there, certainly in his early years, remains uncertain. His time at the Pargeter's farm was at best only a few short years, but this was clearly sufficient to instil in him a basic understanding and a desire to learn more. Barbara Baddeley, on meeting him, had described him as "very well versed in the country" and even in the 1940s and 1950s he had never been without a country home, although this had been a Gypsy caravan in a field for much of the time, which had also been his weekend retreat with Simon, Bay and Barbara.

Until the early 1950s home for Jack had been a number of addresses in London, usually West End properties of one type or another. They ranged from basement flats with just a few rooms to large Edwardian properties with room for both the family and office space dependent on his need at the time. He had often said that "the dream of every young lad who was brought up on a farm, was to get some land." As he became more financially secure in the mid-1950s Jack did precisely this, acquiring a number of cottages and farmhouses, with Jack and Isobel finally settling down in Raven Cottage at Belchalwel in Dorset in 1966. The cottage lay at the bottom of the hill where Tess died in *Tess of the D'Urbervilles*.

As Jack's television work progressed, he found that he frequently needed farm animals to film. He also needed to update his own skills, as much of what he had learnt with the Pargeter's was no longer appropriate in the late 1950s and the 1960s. Raising his own livestock would solve both problems, but it was to be the requirements of the *Out of Town* programmes, which ironically were to prevent him from farming in a real sense; he would be away a lot and Isobel, although extremely supportive of Jack, was not the typical farmer's wife. As a result, they did not have dairy cattle. "You can't even switch the bloody things off on Sunday!" Jack had been heard to say.

Jack had eulogised on many occasions about the secure sense of being rooted that farming the land for generations must have instilled in families as it became their vocation, Only two generations earlier, the Hargreaves family had found themselves in Yorkshire and that had been the case for three generations.

Then Jack's father had begun to work for a wool manufacturer, leaving behind all intentions of working the land. Thus, Jack was denied that feeling of physically belonging and it was not until he was in his fifties that he would have his own herd of beef cattle which they bred themselves with Sussex bulls. It annoyed Jack that Isobel insisted on giving them all names. He had been told that you did not name food animals, only heifer calves which would join the dairy herd and be with you for many years.

Jack also kept chicken (sic) and told the story of the name 'chicken' at any opportunity. Chicken, not 'chickens', was the correct plural. It was a Saxon word like 'children' and 'oxen' and Jack said you could always spot a 'non-countryman' by the way he used it. He always ended the tale by saying the middle classes refer to 'poultry'.

Jack kept his own strain of chicken and put away some forty birds in the freezer each year. The variety was designed to give both a good supply of eggs and a decent amount of meat. It was good all-rounder which Jack had refined over a number of years. The difficulty, as with all strains, is to get the breed to come true each generation. It took him many years to get it right and eventually, on doing so, he had to name it. He chose the name 'Cawthorne' after a village not far from his childhood home in Yorkshire.

Jack also bred food rabbits. For much of his life he had enjoyed netting for rabbits which he had done with the use of a friend's ferret. The advent of myxomatosis and the pressure of work both conspired to bring this pursuit to an end. As he got older and did have the time, he found he was no longer nimble enough to cope with the sport's occasional athletic requirements and so he took advice on breeding. He opted for the Dutch variety when advised that they grew quickly and had beautifully flavoured flesh.

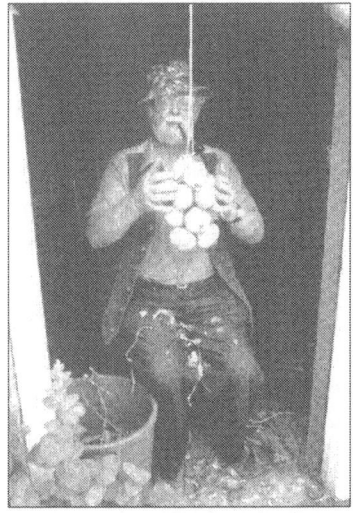

Jack produced a large number of his own vegetables.

He was also a keen market gardener and grew pretty well all of the vegetables they ate. As a rule he would always try something new each year. Due to pressures of work he did require hired help with this for a couple of days a week.

Jack with pack ponies.

Jack's other obsession was ponies and his various carts which they pulled. At the peak of the *Out of Town* series in the 1970s these had grown to quite a considerable number. Although he loved the ponies it was driving them that he most enjoyed. He always had "a feeling that one day the petrol might pack up, and I will be able to continue as we did within a fifteen mile radius when I was a boy." He would spend many hours in his repairing or building from scratch the various carts he drove. Simon, Jack's stepson, recalls regularly being sent to Birmingham to locate various spare parts, pieces of brass, axles or wheels.

Raven Cottage at Belchalwel was a good-sized cottage farmhouse. It had been just one of a number of farms on a country estate which had been broken up after the First World War. Tenants had subsequently bought their own farms from the estate and in a number of instances had then sold them on to third parties. Jack bought the cottage complete with twenty acres. He said, "It was a fairish old mess, and it took me two to three years of very hard work to get it straight." The property came complete with a resident badger which slept near his chicken, but apparently never bothered them. Other local visiting wildlife included spotted woodpeckers and deer.

Jack referred to the cottage as a railway house. It has been built in the 1840s and had been one of the earliest to benefit from the easier movement of materials which the new railways had permitted. Previously roads had been so bad that most houses were built entirely from local materials except in the case of an occasional grand country manor where the owner may have commissioned an expensive stone with little regard for the cost. As the costs came down with better infrastructure, material such as Midland brick and Welsh slate became available in trainloads for the estate builders.

Jack's and Isobel's house had been rebuilt in Victorian times in front of the old one, the farmer moving in when it was finished and its predecessor demolished. You can still to this day see the big arch of clipped yew that had been the front gate, but this now stands at the rear of the house. A small brick area at the back is all that remains of the original building, and it was here that Jack both wrote and recorded numerous tapes. It was covered with elder, a plant which seemed to thrive on old mortar. Jack became known as a regular supplier of elder flower and elder berries in the area.

*

Jack had a particular interest in apples, possibly due to cider being his favourite tipple. He kept a fine orchard where he grew a number of varieties, 'Warrior' and 'Slap my Girdle' being two of his favourites. He used to prepare his own cider from a communal press, which was once filmed for *Out of Town*. Jack's own recipe called for about one third eating apples and two thirds cooking apples. He would allow the juice to ferment naturally in the barrel. He made it in large quantities which he could never manage alone, but there was always someone who would be happy to sample it with him.

Radio presenter Richard Spendlove MBE recalls recording a sound interview with Jack. He had booked himself and his wife into a local hotel for the night and had spent much of the day sampling what Jack called his 'special' cider. As it became time to depart it was clear he was no longer fit to drive and his wife, herself a reluctant driver, had to take the wheel. Richard woke up alone in the car in his own garage. His wife had ignored their hotel reservation and had simply driven home through the night, leaving him in the car to sleep it off.

Larry Skeats, shepherd, writer and landlord of the local village pub, The Trooper, had Jack as a regular customer for many years. The two men became great friends, and Larry made a total of five appearances on *Out of Town*. He was actually the source of many of the items produced by Jack at the end of the programme when he would ask the audience if they knew what they were. He recalls that Jack was always trying to arrange for the two of them to go off to Somerset to buy cider from one of the specialist producers. On a fond note, Jack's picture still hangs in the bar of The Trooper above his usual place.

Jack receiving the runner up award for Pipe Smoker of the Year.
He won it in 1969.

Many of the skills Jack acquired were honed in his world-famous workshop, often referred to as a shed. In addition to building and repairing his carts and buggies there, he also made his fishing tackle, his flies and plaited several hundred horse whips. This shed perhaps earned him his most fitting accolade. He had always been appreciative of his OBE and the title Pipe Smoker of the Year, but the unofficial term 'patron saint of sheds' somehow seems more appropriate as a lasting memory of a man who traditionally began and ended his broadcasts there, surrounded by, as Jack once recounted:

> "A bag of rabbit nets, four old cow bells, a pair of mud pattens, a shooting stick, three bridles, a saddle bracket, seventy pots of paint, a minnow trap, a rat trap, a veterinary grasp, a surgical boot for horses, a bull stick, a dozen china eggs, an echo sounder, landing nets, riding nets, a Channel Island fishing creel, a kostrel (a pottery cider pot), an old spear, a ferret box, three fish tanks, an incubator, bee supplies, fishing rods, lots of horseshoes, decoy pigeons, decoy ducks and the door of an old forge with the various brands burned into it."

Many of Jack's loyal fans were offended when the agony aunt, Virginia Ironside, suggested there was something 'fishy' about the shed. In fact, she was correct. Jack wrote to her editor with the words, 'Who would bring an OB team to the middle of the countryside, when they could do a mock up in the studio?' The television shed was an accurate replica of the original. Alternatives had been costed out and rebuilding the shed had won out over transporting all the required paraphernalia in OB vans to the original. An Art Director had taken many photographs of the original and the place had been painstakingly recreated in a studio. Over the years Jack did have many different 'sheds', his first being in a loft. He called them all his 'Glory Holes.'

It would have been impossible for Jack's life to reflect that of the typical smallholder. He reserved Tuesdays and Thursdays for filming and Wednesdays for the market. He said he did this to keep in touch with thousands of people from the district. They could easily find him, and he could just as easily locate them. If a trip to London was required, it would take place on Friday. If the London trip was not needed, he would go out on various reconnaissance trips checking out suitable locations for filming. Whenever he could he set aside mornings for visiting people he needed to see and doing the jobs he needed to do. Any available afternoons he went into the office to reply to the many letters he received and to complete his paperwork. Weekends were reserved exclusively for work on his smallholding.

*

In later years, when filming was to take up less of his time, Jack settled down to a proper routine. Graham Newland and his wife Sue, together with many other locals, came to know him well as they became regulars at many of the same public houses. Jack described the village pub as a club for the locals and with increasing regularity he could be found at the following places on each day of the week:

Monday: Jack would go to the Sturminster Newton livestock market in the morning and would have lunch in the Royal Oak at Okeford Fitzpaine.

Tuesday: Jack could be found at Larry Skeat's pub, The Trooper, in Stourton Caundle.

Wednesday: Usually he could be found in The Crown Inn at Ibberton, the closest pub to his home and the place where his personal cider mug was kept. Although the landlord at that time used to make a beef curry which Jack liked very much, he would sometimes supply his own mutton and ask John, the landlord, to make a special lamb curry which was his absolute all-time favourite. Graham Newland remembers the mother of the landlady used to joke about not bothering to put an ashtray on Jack's table because he always used to tap his pipe out on the heel of his boot or the floor and never once did he use an ashtray!

Thursday: He would be at the Three Elms at North Wootton. Jack liked the cider there, which was made at Pass Vale Farm, Burrow Hill, in Somerset.

Friday: He would lunch at Blackmore Vale Inn at Marnhull. Jack enjoyed the steaks and traditional cider there. He said at the time that their steaks were the best in Dorset. He always ate the Parisian Sirloin.

Saturday and Sunday: Jack and Isobel could be found at The Crown Inn at Ibberton. Jack would again enjoy one of his favourite curries and wash it down with a pint or two of traditional cider.

Not averse to a drop of beer, Jack samples a pint of Huntsman brewed by Eldridge Pope of Dorchester.

In order to answer any questions regarding Jack Hargreaves's seemingly unassailable position as a voice of authority on all matters rural we must perhaps take something of a leap of faith. The man was born in London and he spent a lot of time there. His aspirations were truly rural, but the requirements on his time, if he was to communicate its wonders, were very much urban. Yet it was his strength as a voice of introduction to these topics which raised him beyond the level of the ordinary. He always remained somewhat concerned about his own expertise and the mantle he wore as everyone's favourite country uncle.

If we ask ourselves "Did we trust him?" then the answer becomes a little clearer. He really did awaken within us an interest in traditions which were often on their way out and if he had not done so we would never have been aware that they ever had existed and that at one time they had been a source of income and livelihood for many of our forebears. It was perhaps Jack's greatest feat that, on the television programme *How* it was never even realised by the hundreds of thousands of viewers who tuned in each week that Jack Hargreaves was an executive behind the scenes whose boardroom tactics had brought about the programme's realisation; he was simply the bloke brought in because he knew a lot about the traditions of rural life and we knew it because he had the answers and if they had come from anyone else we might not have taken the trouble to listen.

Chapter 10
A Jack of All Trades

Jack's skills as an all rounder were developed as needed. Sometimes they were leisure pursuits, at other times they were sporting interests. Throughout his early life his real interests had grown in the countryside and this had encompassed both leisure and necessity; the shotgun and the rod being an example of both, and use of the boat coming as an extension of the rod. Jack has always been both an innovator and a great learner and his encounters with the best in both shooting and fishing had certainly added to his own natural abilities. These pursuits all formed the basis of many features on his various television programmes, but his earliest break as a radio broadcaster came as a result of his role as librarian of the Piscatorial Society, itself a high accolade and a tribute to his then achievements and commitment to the sport.

Jack and Fishing

Jack made only one claim about his fishing: he said that out of some two million anglers in the UK, most of them only ever enjoyed one single type of fishing. They specialised as wet fly, dry fly, sea anglers, salmon fishermen or tope fishermen; so many indeed, all fiercely loyal to their own specialisations and all too often openly hostile to anyone else's. Jack's claim did not encompass the size of his catches or indeed the legendary ones which might have got away; merely the fact that he might have been the only true all rounder in the angling world.

He also made another claim which may well remain undisputed even to this day; that he was the only person ever to make a hundred television films about fishing.

His passion went back to his early youth. He had been taught by his uncle and had certainly acquired his skills well before his meeting with Victor Pargeter who would have given him little encouragement anyway as he considered fishing a complete waste of time. He did fish as a boy both in Yorkshire with his uncle and at the Pargeter's farm and then as a youth while at school in London. By the time he had left to study at university he was already an accomplished coarse fisherman. Throughout the 1930s fishing was always his release from the stress of both his occupation and his increasingly troubled marriage.

Jack's earliest fishing took place on the moor fed streams near Huddersfield. Their waters were cold, often brown, swollen by rain, acidic from the peat of the moor lands they passed through and lacking in the invertebrate life needed to nurture the kind of fish he would catch in later years on the great chalk streams of the South. Trout grew to only half a pound in weight and Jack said on more than one occasion that if you added a glass of water from the River Calder to the Hampshire Avon the mixture would fizz.

As with all things, Jack did not merely wish to participate but went into the history of the sport, its technology and its science. It was not that old as a popular sport, although it was centuries old as a pastime of the wealthy and the nobility. Most of its developments and innovations took place either in the pre-Victorian period or during Jack's own lifetime when money was thrown into research in order to satisfy the new breed of keen hobby fishermen. He had studied these developments in both tackle and technique in some detail and spent considerable time with some of the country's finest.

For many years Jack had fished the Kennett, and it had become familiar to him. Every year he had taken a boat and drifted downstream, making a note of every weed and every fallen tree trunk. He had a perfect mental picture of what was happening at any one time, and he knew where to find the perch, the chub, the trout or the grayling, but his real education began when filming called for him to fish in unknown waters. He said, "I felt like a blind man on the new waters, and I developed a great admiration for the match fisherman who can go to strange places and still come home with a prize." He went on to say that it was only in filming fishing programmes that he got to know the difference between a good and a great fisherman.

He also became aware as he travelled from river to river that the same species of fish had completely different tastes as far as bait was concerned; similarly, their habits would be entirely different dependent on the water quality, current or flow. On the Kennett he knew that large roach were caught using maggots but on the Stour, Jack filmed Owen Wentworth, the postman and master fishing coach, catching large roach over two pounds in weight, using bread. One day they decided to use the Stour as an experiment and both Jack and Owen fished from the same boat, Jack using maggots and Owen using bread. For an hour and a half

Jack caught nothing while Owen caught many. They then swapped bait and Jack caught many while Owen's tally fell to nought. It is perhaps worth noting that in later years Jack stopped using bread because he believed, as a pipe smoker, that the tobacco on his fingers tainted the bread. He referred to maggots as 'smoker's bait' because they stank so much it masked the tobacco odour.

Jack fished the River Avon in his cathedral-hulled punt.

Jack loved to fish both the Stour and its twin sister, the Hampshire Avon. He regarded the Dorset Stour as the finest coarse fishing river in England. Both merged together at the Christchurch Priory and went on to share a common estuary but were wholly different prior to their becoming one. The Stour rises in a clay valley, a characteristic of clay being that it is impervious to water. Consequently, rain fills the river rapidly and it has a tendency to flood when the rain is heavy. The Hampshire Avon rises in the chalk of Salisbury Plain and filters through the meadows. In contrast it rarely floods, the rainfall simply soaking through the porous chalk and effectively filtering off into the underground water system.

In practice this meant that the two rivers had to be fished in entirely different ways. As it would often be in flood, the Stour would need an angler of almost prophetic insight to judge the flow and height of the water. The Hampshire Avon, by contrast, would be more or less consistent. It has been said, "A man could come at almost any time of the year and find it fishable."

Jack, in common with other writers on the subject, had written affectionately of the Hampshire Avon and the other great chalk streams of the South. He wrote, 'From Beachy Head up through Hampshire and Berkshire and on into Wiltshire, past Stonehenge, run the chalk hills, and when the rain falls on chalk something different happens from when it falls on the rock of the mountains or the clay or the loams of the lowlands. The chalk acts as a sponge. These are the great springs of Southern England; the River Test, the River Itchen, the Hampshire Avon and their tributaries.' The numerous eulogies paid to these rivers by anglers over the years have elevated them to the mythical status of a Piscatorial Holy Grail.

On the Stour, a big part of the day's fishing is ruled by the thermometer. It was Owen who showed Jack exactly why temperature mattered so much. Below thirty-eight degrees Fahrenheit they caught nothing, but at thirty-nine Owen predicted they would catch chub and they did. At forty degrees Fahrenheit he suggested they would catch roach and was again proved correct. Of course, the same would apply to the Hampshire Avon, but given the variations in temperature the influx of floodwater would create in the Stour, the skill needed to meet its challenges would be somewhat greater.

Jack enjoying a day of coarse fishing.

Jack had learned to coarse fish back in the days when a large catch would end up in a trip to the taxidermist to convert it into a trophy. His earliest days were spent fishing for roach, a fish once believed to live in greater numbers than people in England. It varied across the UK not only in size and weight, but also in shape. In some places a good catch would weigh in at just half a pound, whereas in others it would exceed two pounds. He had spent long hours studying the banks of the Kennett and simply watching the shoals of roach, fascinated how they broke down into smaller fish at the front and rather higher than the larger ones which lay somewhat lower and further to the back. They also fed in a different manner; the smaller ones were impetuous and rushed to feed, but the larger fish seemed more calculating and deliberate.

Jack also noted the roach was sensitive to light. A friend went out with Jack once to measure exactly how sensitive they were using a light meter, although their eventual conclusion that it was 'very sensitive' did not earn their experiment a lasting place in the annals of science. Jack did tell a story though about a witness called to give evidence in a court case concerning a somewhat grizzly crime. An attempt was made to discredit him by asking what he was doing about at such an unearthly hour. He simply answered, "My Lord, I am a roach fisherman!" which apparently placed his presence there beyond suspicion.

The first fish caught by Jack using a fly was a dace. He described it as the finest of all fish to catch in this manner and said on his record, *Know Your Fish*, "You could drop your fly directly in the middle of the shoal and as long as you keep missing, they'll keep coming." A German had once measured the speed of freshwater fish and had found the dace to be the quickest with a speed of approximately two metres per second. It is certainly more streamlined than a roach and measured in at four times faster than a carp. Jack reckoned you had to be able to strike most of the dace which nibbled at your bait before you could call yourself a fisherman, no mean feat as it always seemed capable of recognising the hook in the middle of the bait. To get over this problem Jack would sometimes fill a 16's hook with four or five maggots. Ever the realist, he added, "But then you might lose some the other way because the hook would be so masked."

Jack paid little attention to the weight of his catches and kept his scales at the very bottom of his bag. "I'm not into the numbers game," he said. "I like fish and the sport of fishing them." That said, he did for a short time hold the record for the biggest tope, although his record only stood for a couple of days. He also made an attempt to join the Ton-up club, fishing for Atlantic Skate in Northern Scotland where catches regularly weigh in at over one hundred pounds. He did manage to hook one, but his line snapped, and his attempt ended without success.

Ever curious about beliefs and lore, Jack was interested in the rhyme 'When the wind is in the West then the fishes bite the best; when the wind is in the East then the fishes bite the least.' He was certain that the fish had no sense of either east or west, but he did have a theory about barometric pressure and felt it might be the real basis for the adage as easterly winds are associated with high pressure. Would a build-up of high pressure put off bottom feeding fish such as chub? Although he did begin to keep records, he knew his chances of ever proving anything were slim.

Over the years Jack embraced many advances in fishing technology affecting both rod and line but the sport to benefit most from these developments was that of fly fishing. He had written of the sport's early days when 'the Houghton Club on the River Test, with their tented pavilions set up beside the waters and the innumerable servants serving meals and drinks, stood by the waterside in their beaver hats and caught trout with an imitation of the mayfly, tied with the hackle feathers of the French Partridge. But they were doing it by a means known as 'dapping'. They had very tall rods from the end of which hung a light blowline of floss silk which would be tossed in any breeze and by getting their backs to the wind they were able to aim the artificial fly as it tossed in the breeze on the end of the blowline until it was hovering over the mouth of a rising trout and then drop it on his nose.'

They had not then known how to cast a dry fly without the aid of a breeze and certainly not into the breeze itself, due to rod technology, the lightness of the material from which the line was manufactured and the virtual weightlessness of the fly itself. The development of tapered line made casting considerably easier as it could be cast much further irrespective of the prevailing wind conditions.

The other prohibitive factor affecting fly fishing, certainly in the early days of the *Out of Town* series, was the cost of participation; it was a well-to-do sport. Fishing rights on stretches of water were changing hands for tens of thousands of pounds per mile even in the early sixties, and syndicates of fishermen were paying hundreds of pounds a year for what might amount to no more than a dozen days fishing each year. Jack reckoned the cost to be about five pounds per fish, which was then approximately half a week's wage for most people.

Although Jack was keen to welcome developments in technology, he was sometimes less appreciative of the trends in fishing. He believed the trout to be a noble fish and all fish below it were common. He had caught his first trout with a fly on the Lambourn. He had written, 'It is held by those who fish for the brown trout with the dry fly in the chalk waters of

Southern England - and grudgingly admitted by other fishermen - that theirs is the highest angling art.' Soon everyone wanted to do it and helping them to do so became big business. Trout were thus raised in tanks and fed artificially before being dumped into lakes or rivers; often far too many for the waters to cope with naturally. Because they were perpetually hungry, they would snap at virtually anything, but also, because they were used to being fed by having food thrown in, they were actually very trusting. Jack could not see the sport in this and believed that any true angler should prefer a truly wild fish.

Jack believed in the totemic relationship between fisherman and fish, and wrote, 'Once a fish is caught the game is over. The art is in the outwitting." To catch a trout which you had not known was there, he viewed as a disgrace, describing the highest virtue as being available to the fisherman who caught his trout "on a perfect imitation of the very fly on which it is at that moment feeding.'

Although Jack was highly rated as a fly spinner, he was at least as good a yarn spinner. He once told a tale in Faber and Faber's *Best Fishing Stories* about a time he went fishing while on leave during the Second World War. He had been within cycling distance of the Hampshire Avon and had borrowed an army bicycle to get there. He was dismayed to find that the river, unusually, was in flood, as he knew that the fish did not like flood water. He realised, however, that a lady who lived a couple of miles downstream happened to have a side stream running on to her land. An inspired thought occurred to him that the fish would probably be sheltering there. The stream ended in a sluice which in turn fed a deep pool.

Jack's inspired guess paid off and he caught roach, grayling, chub and dace in very larger numbers, so much so that his net was completely full. The pool itself had at one time been a feeder for a large old eel house whose keeper occupied the cottage close by and, as Jack did not wish to return the fish directly into the pool, he arranged to store them in the tanks of the eel house. He then turned his attention to pulling yet more chub from the water, which he added to those already in the eel tank.

The keeper offered to return the fish himself on the following day, saying that he would normally wait for a day to let them normalise before doing so. Jack, deferring but not understanding the keeper's words, gave him a generous tip and cycled back to camp, overjoyed with both the day's fishing and his ingenuity in overcoming the problem of floodwater.

The following morning Jack cycled off to a shop to buy some cigarettes and noticed a handsome pony and trap outside the shop. Inside was the keeper selling his bumper catch from the day before. They both offered each other an embarrassed 'Good Morning'.

It was only through television that Jack learned that sea fishing could be every bit as skilful and absorbing as fishing on a river. He had viewed sea fishing as being a game of chance with nothing more than a 'just chuck it and see' attitude. He felt this had been confirmed during one of Southern Television's Sea Fishing Competitions where he had seen some three hundred or so competitors in deck chairs with belled rods, falling asleep as they waited. Jack and his cameraman walked a long way towards a man with his rod in his hand and his bait sheltered from the sun. Just by looking at him Jack decided he would be the winner and, through watching him, he learned a little about the tides, the behaviour of the fish and how they fed with regard to the tides and the state of the sea.

Filming *Out of Town* was to profoundly change Jack's attitude to the sea in many respects. He had spent many series fishing on lakes and rivers before he first ventured out to sea, but a letter from Gerald Ashton Smith, the Commodore of Lymington Sea Angling Association, was to change all that. He had told Jack that it was all very good fishing in rivers, but it was high time he turned his attention to sea fishing. The letter was so good that Jack paid him a visit, and by the following weekend, they were at sea in an old naval cutter.

Jack described the year that followed as "the most intensive education about the sea." He learned from dozens of sea anglers, some cod men, others favouring bass, and he went out in all kinds of boats in all kinds of weather. He was certain he was nowhere near learning everything about sea fishing, but said, "I have fished at sea so much that I have become an expert in the art and science of seasickness." He maintained that the first lesson was to learn not to be ashamed of being seasick! He met weekend sailors immune to it and world class single-handed sailors who were always 'sick as a dog' for days.

Jack found that sleep was the best way of keeping seasickness at bay and a good night's sleep would alleviate most of the problems. He also discovered that he was never seasick when a boat was underway but became badly sick when it stopped at anchor. Similarly, he noted that food was important and would begin to eat his lunch as soon as he began to feel ill. In fact, Jack took Ollie Kite out to sea, as the famed fly fisherman had caught many fish in both lakes and rivers but never at sea. The weather was awful and everyone on the boat was horrendously seasick, except Ollie who walked with the assuredness of being on dry land. The trip provided no shots as the cameraman they had taken remained green-faced at the bottom of the boat without shooting an inch of film.

Although Jack's admiration for the skills of sea fishing did greatly improve, he remained at heart a man who chose to do it inland, possibly due to his dislike of seasickness.

*

He remained for many years a member of the Piscatorial Society or, as he wrote in *The Field* in 1974, 'the club of harmonious fly fishermen.' The Society has long had an undeservedly austere reputation. It was formed in 1836 in a public house with the aim of encouraging harmonious and social conversation and Jack fitted in right away. He became their librarian in 1950. The job entailed doing some much needed work.

He took it upon himself to catalogue each of the two thousand books and read hundreds of them, many more than once. He noticed that much of the literature on the subject was 'mutually plagiaristic'. He arranged for postal delivery of the books to the membership so that their knowledge would be spread and even opened his own home at weekends if anyone wished to use it as a collection point. He collected more books and cased them with overhead lighting; all beautifully arranged at his own home in Bagnor. Once he had finished the cataloguing he offered for sale 'a valuable collection of angling books being the surplus resulting from the amalgamation of the libraries of the Piscatorial Society and Gresham Angling Society.' Among them were the following notable collections and books, many now worth astronomical sums if ever they were to come on to the open market:

'Seventeen volumes of *The New Sporting Magazine* from May 1831 to November 1839. These include the works of Nimrod and in twenty instalments, The Adventures of the Handley Cross Hounds.' Jack wanted seventeen guineas.

'A Treatyse of Fysshynge with an Angle by Dame Juliana Berners, being

a facsimile reproduction of the first book on the subject of fishing printed in England by Wynkin de Worde at Westminster in 1496. Bound in tooled parchment at four pounds.'

'The Compleat Angler, Hawkins, First Edition 1760. Five pounds.'

Perhaps the most recognised author for the non-fisherman and youngsters alike was Sir Humphrey Davy's *Salmonia*, or *Days and Nights of Fly Fishing* which sold for two pounds and ten shillings.

In 1958 Jack agreed to continue as the society's librarian until they could acquire their own premises and secure someone to do the job full time. Some of the books were extremely valuable and were not to be taken away, so a permanent home where members could consult them was the only solution.

Jack's reading on the subject of fishing led him to make a number of interesting discoveries, one of which was the fact that Isaak Walton's *Compleat Angler* had run to more editions than any other work in the English language except for the Bible. Jack described the book, written in old English, as very boring, but in spite of this the society had every single edition on its shelves.

Over the years the membership of the Piscatorial Society has read like a who's who of the British establishment. As a member Jack would have rubbed shoulders with MPs, QCs, OBEs, KBEs, as well as the odd High Court Judge, not to mention a few Lords and presumably some of Jack's own friends from both the world of broadcasting and advertising. Jack remained a fishing member throughout the 1960s but eventually reduced his role to that of a non-fishing member, due mainly to his filming commitments, finally leaving altogether in 1978. His absence was noted and Dr. Thirlaway, the society president, wrote to him saying, 'Do come back! It's only a tenner, and we should love to entertain you in our rod room.'

*

At the time of Jack's first marriage, during the early 1930s the government had built a railway line through the Chilterns and beyond. In a short time, the route had become populated by dormitory towns and as they grew up, so the rivers began to die; the Misbourne, the Gade and the Colne, all of them as a result of both pollution and a lack of water. Many years later Jack wrote retrospectively in *The Field* that this had been a time when "the skids were under us." The totemic relationship he believed existed between fisherman and fish was as nothing when compared to the relationship between fisherman and stream. Without the waters the sport would indeed be dead!

The fate of the Misbourne was especially sad for Jack. He had written, 'Through the clear water - never flooding and never dwindling away - you could see the bright gravel and the clean silt at the roots of the trailing water plants. The scene was garlanded with ranunculuses and comfrey and meadowsweet. The stream was alive with minnows and shrimp and water fleas, together with dozens of species of ephemera and sedge flies. They all fed the native brown trout, sometimes to extraordinary weights for the size of the stream. On one of these streams, the little River Misbourne, I first learned to cast a dry fly.' How could a river which had run its course for so many millennia simply disappear in a matter of a few years?

In the 1930s with the threat of invasion and concerns as to how the nation might feed itself, the planners sanctioned not only the further removal of water from these rivers but also commenced the wholesale clearance of wetland around the rivers in order to grow crops. These crops, in turn, needed irrigation from the rivers, drawing yet more water from the system and the process continued after the war as the dormitory towns continued to grow and the efforts of farmers to feed the new residents called for yet more water.

Jack went to see a Water Authority engineer in the late 1950s and was informed that "three more bore holes in the Kennett region would finish the summer flow of this river for good."

The cost of all these new settlements had to be paid for, but a new form of currency was being spent. The new currency was water, without which none of them could have existed and the chalk over which these rivers flowed had been the reason for their demise. It was a very cheap form of filtration. Jack raised his concerns about the Allen with the planners, asking them where they were piping the water that they were taking from the headwaters of the river. They replied that it was going to Bournemouth and Poole. "But that's exactly where it is going anyway. Why don't you collect it from down there?" They told him, "If we took it from down there it would have to be purified and that would be very expensive."

Jack contacted all the Water Authorities with regard to the concerns of the fishing community. He wished to know how they could improve the situation for both anglers and wildlife. They replied to the effect that they had just one brief: to double the supply of water to the cities in the next ten years. Jack responded with, 'The rise of water consumption in the Entitlement Society, and the Technological World that it supported, was colossal. Bathrooms, showers, swimming pools and Jacuzzis. Street washers for growing cities. Power hoses for cleaning lorries daily. Coolers for new power stations. Washing machines by the million. And now, since time at the sink was 'infra dig' (Latin for below one's dignity) in the Entitlement Society, the greedy dishwasher, the ultimate liberator.'

For the consummate fisherman such as Jack, and the birdwatchers and botanists, there were fatalities to mourn. The top half of the River Pang dried, the Meon virtually disappeared, and the Allen, once famed for its trout, was reduced to a trickle. The Tarrant was ruined by a single bore hole and the Piddle dried up in the summer. Jack described the water as going from the chalk straight into the dishwasher system. He came to refer to this period which saw the demise of many of the nation's great rivers as the 'Great Dishwasher Murders.'

After he had ended his association with all other fishing groups, Jack chose to remain with High Hall which owned a section of the Allen for three quarters of a mile downstream of Fitches Bridge. He had made a number of films on this river with Owen Wentworth and the leader of the syndicate, John Bass. Indeed, it was to John Bass that Jack wrote a letter in 1990 when a fight was taking place to stop the extraction of water from the river by the local water company. His letter went as follows:

```
28th May, 1990

Dear John,

I wouldn't want to seem to grumble after all the joy I have
had on the Allen under your leadership; but I must write
to say that my several visits to the river this season have
been utterly saddening. It is a ruin of the river we knew
twenty years ago.

Of course, we have seen it happening gradually, but
recently there seemed to be a ray of hope. Even the 'green'
groups said it was a move in the right direction that
independent    supervisory    organisations    were    being
appointed.
```

The whole thing proved to be just a parliamentary demonstration for the benefit of the media which was then left to a disingenuous bureaucracy. These controlling authorities are now saying that they are prevented by lack of budget and staff from carrying out the ecological studies that they needs must do before they can set standards. In the meanwhile their replies to angler's letters studiously avoid the matters of pollution and extraction.

It is too late for these evasive studies. There are plenty of good fishermen-naturalists who have known the rivers for fifty years who can give evidence of what has happened ecologically. I can tell you what has happened to the River Allen - as follows!

The average water level is down by 60% of what it was fifteen years ago. There are no water voles and their homes are dried out two feet above the water. There is an occasional moorhen but no coots or dabchicks. The flocks of swallows and martins no longer come down to hawk the hatches of olive flies. There are no olives because there is no green weed in the river. The water runs shallow over a dirty gravel bed that is soiled with undesirable algae. This year I have seen only two hatches of fly - a few mayfly and some sedges, both silt bred creatures. There are very few wild fish - not even minnows - except from the annual migration of grayling from below. It is a rare thing to come upon a trout below stock size.

He who runs may read. We do not need the help of any more recently graduated BScs wandering bemusedly with nets and bottles. We need some tough, politically sophisticated executives. And we need them to be supported with resources and, above all, given a revision of the Act which allows the undertakings to sue for damages if they are told not to extract water.

Of course, extraction is the heart of the matter. At its old strength the Allen could probably stand up to what is being put into it - whether from paper mills or farm sprays and effluents - but as the level falls the solution of pollutants gets stronger and stronger.

Since prehistoric times the waters of the Allen have flowed into the sea at Bournemouth Bay. Now they are extracted from the high chalk and sent straight to Bournemouth and Poole to avoid the cost of cleaning.

Cost? I suppose they are concerned with the cost of providing millions of gallons at a silly price to women working washing-machines and fat men sitting in Jacuzzis and still giving a return to shareholders.

The real cost is the death of a river that God made and that Wilson Stephens, only fifteen years ago, described in his book as the most perfect of all small chalk streams.

I suppose that those who now tell us the economy has never been in better shape would smile at the passion I am unable to keep out of this letter. I am reminded of the fierce Scottish padre we had in the army. He would stand and watch us tumbling into the liberty wagons at closing time. "Ye may giggle! Ye may giggle!" he used to shout. "But ye're all bound for Hell!"

Kind regards,
Jack Hargreaves, OBE
Fisherman and Country Broadcaster.

*

Jack's work on the River Allen brought many requests for him to add his weight to similar struggles by other societies. By now he was over eighty and found it increasingly difficult to find the energy to meet these demands. He was committed to all the efforts of all the nation's fishing societies faced with similar plights, particularly the River Mole Preservation Association. He had written in *The Field* magazine in the strongest terms about the states of these rivers and, together with other younger people such as Tony Jacques, Bill Humphries and Richard Slocock, had been able to convince the National Rivers Authority to slow down the extraction of waters from the chalk streams of the South, leaving them in a still vulnerable but safer position.

Jack and Boats

Although he could still sail, Jack was never much of a sailor, preferring powered vessels as a means of reaching any destination quickly. His real interest lay in building and renovating vessels, with Simon as the beneficiary when it came to using them. Jack's first venture was the building of a dinghy for Simon, a fairly unremarkable craft suitable for either a lake or a reasonably calm river. The most remarkable thing about the boat, though, was its place of construction, the offices of *Lilliput* magazine. The venture became something of a joke among Jack's fellow scribes as they congregated for a 'swift half' in the pubs of Fleet Street.

Jack's next venture was also to undergo its construction in the offices of

Lilliput where he knew he could justify it to the senior management by taking photographs at various stages and writing an article about it for the magazine. This project was complete with the help of Colin Willock and was to be a gun punt for the purpose of wildfowling to which he been introduced by Colin on the River Medway. As its construction progressed, so did Jack's own interest in the technology of boat building and he became interested in both marine ply and the amazing achievements of aircraft manufacturers with wood.

A gun punt was designed to float silently towards swimming wildfowl. A single gun attached to the vessel would then be used to shoot the resting birds. The problem with this project was that they had no plans to guide them. Jack did a lot of research using old sporting books, and from photographs and descriptions they eventually managed to get an idea of the boat they wished to build.

Jack drew up plans and then, using stepson Simon's fretsaw, he cut out a model of what the boat should look like. The entire frame was made of plywood and the sides and the bottom were cardboard. Unfortunately, the painting process warped the cardboard so it did not look quite as professional as they had hoped, but it certainly did impress the staff at the office as it took pride of place on Colin's desk.

The actual punt was built in Jack's loft among old lamp stands and bicycles. He lived in an old school house at the time and the loft doubled as his workshop. His neighbour, the actor Michael Hordern, came in whenever he could to help, relating stories of the difficulties of life in the entertainment industry. He seemed to have been cast in a Shakespearean adaptation alongside Richard Burton and Elizabeth Taylor and was apparently finding the antics of these love-struck, self-destructive people very difficult to cope with.

When completed, the punt, designed to transport two men, their equipment and a large gun, proved too big to move from the loft by the conventional exit and a part of a wall had to be demolished to allow its removal. They named it 'Sneak' in anticipation of its silent stalking abilities and painted it in a traditional kittiwake grey. Jack and Colin used it frequently over a period of five or so years. Colin said, "We never shot a huge amount, but then you never do." He actually wrote the adventure into a book which he called *The Gun Punt*.

The gun punt in use.

A larger project came with the chance to buy an old ship's lifeboat at the time large numbers were coming onto the market due to many being decommissioned. They made ideal pleasure craft and as the motors had usually been well maintained they were great value for money. This particular one was brought back to their home at Bagnor and stripped down on the street. Weekends were spent filling, fixing and scraping down the bare wood, after which a cabin was put on and painted to look like new. The boat was christened 'Blackbird' after the local pub which still remains today and the boat was taken to Preddy's Head to be launched.

Jack on a sea fishing trip, probably on Blackbird.

Jack also acquired a sailing boat in 1960. She was a gaff rigged nineteen-foot cutter named 'Hoppy' after the daughter of a neighbour. She had been a retirement vessel for an old sea captain and had needed rather a lot of work. Jack had scraped her, cleaned her out, repaired the clinker-built hull and put a cabin on her. She was always regarded as being Simon Baddeley's boat, although Jack used her for both filming and entertainment, sometimes taking both Judy Hogg and their daughter Polly out on trips on the Solent.

Jack sailing Hoppy.

At about this time Jack began to ponder on the possibilities of building a boat which might encompass a number of attributes not found in yachts. His main concerns were that it should be cheap, easy to sail and capable of fulfilling a weekend's sailing requirements, but also that it should be fully able to cope with the challenges of the world's major oceans.

At this time Jack met Denys Rayner, a former war time officer with an exemplary and groundbreaking record in the Royal Navy Reserve. He had been given his own ship command with the first long fo'c'sle corvette, HMS *Verbena* (Pennant K85) and had been decorated. He had managed to survive shipwreck due to enemy action and later sank two U-boats. After the war he raised pigs and had started to build small family sailing boats 'of distinctive style' at the village of Donnington near Newbury.

As with all wars the Second World War had been a time of innovation, and advances in new epoxy bonding techniques had made plywood a reliable material for boat building even when constantly immersed in water. Using a mahogany frame and the new WPB (water boiling point) plywood, commonly called marine ply, Rayner had built a twenty-foot hard chine bilge keel gunter rigged sloop called 'The Westcoaster'. It was a huge boat designed for the difficult waters of the Bristol Channel with headroom for tall men incorporating a design which enhanced its sleek appearance by disguising the reverse sheer.

Jack and Denys Rayner entered into collaboration with Jack providing a wish list of improvements and design ideas based on the requirements of the hobby sailor and Denys taking on the challenge of achieving them. The result was 'The Westerly Corvette', a five-ton sloop with full standing headroom. Only two of the boats were ever built with Jack hinself buying one. He wanted to call her 'Mayfly' but was dismayed to find the name was already in use so he opted for the name 'Danica', the Mayfly's scientific name.

Simon Baddeley advertised in the national press for a skipper to teach him how to sail *Danica* on a trip to the Mediterranean, the Greek islands and Athens via the Bay of Biscay and the French inland waterway system. This resulted in a six-month tour with Chris Jameson which verified her sea worthiness. She returned a little bumped and scraped, but perfectly sound, even overcoming the hostility of a force ten gale in the Bay of Biscay during the return journey.

Denys Rayner moved from using marine ply to using fibre glass for the building of his boats. Both he and Jack had become fascinated with the challenge of bending marine ply under steam with a view to overcoming the limitation of its only bending one dimensionally, thus creating a 'chine' or a sharp line where two pieces met. Fibre glass presented no such problem and his new Westerley 22 became very popular indeed. Its twin keels permitted the boat to be brought in only a few yards from shore which made it the ideal vessel for island hopping. Jack bought one which he called 'Young Tiger' after his television series. Both he and Stan Bréhaut filmed her from Hoppy as she left the south coast to cross the Atlantic with Simon as skipper in his own right accompanied by a university friend, Susanna, filling in as crew. Sadly Hoppy, although she had been beautifully finished by Jack, had been left on mud for some years and as a result she nearly sank as they filmed.

Jack repaired her and sold her on.

Jack on board the Young Tiger on Canal de Midi, 1965.

Simon and Susanna's trip took them to the West Indies via Las Palmas de Gran Canaria, a distance of some two thousand and nine hundred miles per day. On reaching Bridgetown, Simon received a letter from Denys Rayner dated the fourteenth December 1965. It said, 'Welcome to the Caribbean and well done! I think this is a justified remark because if you do not get this letter you won't have done so well! I am glad you have Susanna with you. I shall of course calm down anyone who gets jumpy, because I have complete confidence in you and the boat.'

For the journey the boat had been jam packed with navigational equipment and a specially designed new autopilot system that Jack was interested in filming for a future *Out of Town* programme. Having earlier placed considerable emphasis on both the financial and organisational powers of Isobel, it is worth noting that Simon had to account for all these items ranging from sextants, compasses, anchors and so on, signing for each on a chit to be retained in her records.

The journey had been yet another test for Denys Rayner's abilities as a boat builder. His vessels had not yet been given a Lloyds Certification, fibre-glass still being in its infancy and its durability still viewed as uncertain. It is interesting to note, though, that prior to his association with Jack, a similar boat cost upwards of six thousand pounds to buy, but the Westerley 22 was priced at one thousand eight hundred pounds, was clearly safe, came complete with a trailer and included the cost of delivery - in other words Jack's wish list had effectively been met. The Westerley 22 was helping to bring sailing to the masses, and this fact was not appreciated by all members of the sailing establishment, with the result that it was made clear that Denys Rayner would no longer be welcomed at a well-known yachting club.

Jack and Guns

Jack loved shooting, but he did not learn to do so properly until he was called up to fight in the Second World War. Along with so many others he was presented with an ordinary lee Enfield rifle. He had used a 'four-ten' (.410) at the Pargeter's to shoot the odd pigeon or rabbit but had not yet distinguished himself. At Sandhurst he took the small arms course as a young officer and received his service revolver. His real training, though, involved him shooting from tanks, something he would not have considered sporting for day to day wildfowling or rough shooting.

Jack had learned the basic rules of shooting from Victor Pargeter, including safety, not returning to the farm with a loaded gun, not mixing bore sizes and cartridges. It was only after he moved to London that he became proficient, refining his abilities at the West London Shooting School which he attended for the first time in the 1930s. He continued to do so on and off for the next twenty years.

Jack described his first gun as an old hand-me-down Purdy, but it was not among those he owned in later life. His shotgun licence listed two .410 single barrels, an Army and Navy and an Investarm. He also had two twelve bores, a single barrelled Savage and a double-barrelled Webley and Scott, the latter being the one most likely to accompany him on a shoot.

Jack not only learned to shoot, he learned a lot about guns too, from American repeating shotguns to antique four bore wildfowling weapons. He was also quite prepared to have a go at making his own guns. In the 1950s both he and his colleague Colin Willock set out to make a gun for the gun punt they had built together. Again, they viewed the project as pretty much in line with their roles on the magazine as it had traditionally been a required read for gentlemen shooters and was also a magnet for the various gunsmiths and gun shops, all of whom flocked around Jack and Colin in the hope of getting a few precious words about their products in the magazine's editorial.

At Jack's insistence they decided the ideal gun for the punt would be a six bore. It would have to be strapped into position and tied over the bow of the boat to allow it to take the force of the recoil. They both chipped in to buy such a gun, but then decided it was not big enough for their needs. Thomas Bland, the wildfowler's gunsmith, was at that time situated on the Strand in London and became very interested in the project, lending them a Bland four bore which Colin took out to Stoke Ooze for a test firing.

He shot at several flights of widgeon without actually hitting any. Also, the recoil of the gun spun him round several times and the amount of powder needed to fire the shot from a four-bore gun made it a very cumbersome weapon; this particular one weighed in at seventeen pounds. The term 'bore', as in twelve bore, six bore and so forth, refers to the fraction of a pound of lead shot that will precisely fill the bore of the gun. Thus, a twelve bore will take one twelfth of a pound of lead shot and a four bore will take a quarter of a pound. Consequently, the latter needs an awful lot more energy to throw its shot out of the gun with deadly velocity and this extra energy comes from larger cartridges containing more powder. In order to contain the extra force safely, the gun must be of significantly greater physical strength.

Jack considered buying a length of steel and having it bored out. He thought of creating a double four, meaning two barrels, each of four bore, propelling half a pound of shot at a time. The dimensions of the tube would have to be an inch bore with sides three quarters of an inch thick. It could be fed from a screw breech. They managed to find such a piece of metal from Tube Investments in Birmingham but not without considerable expense and having it transported to London cost them a fortune. They were also sent an old muzzle loading four bore punt gun, for which they paid ten pounds, then well in excess of the average weekly wage. This beast had clearly seen better days, and they decided to have it tested before firing it themselves.

The inside of the gun was severely pitted; years of damp and use had taken their toll. The bore had to be cleaned, which was a substantial and expensive job. When it finally went to the proving shop, the gun, on firing, split down a fault line. It had been a much better option to explode the gun in the sand of a test bed than to have it take a hole out of the bottom of their new punt. Their search, however, would have to begin again.

The day after this setback, Jack appeared carrying a Reilly four bore gun which he had bought from a man at Downham Market for £20. It had recently been proved and was ready for use. The six foot long gun certainly turned a few heads in the *Lilliput* offices when they laid it on the floor to find its balancing point by propping it on a few telephone directories.

The Reilly was thoroughly tested by Jack and Colin, first at the West London Shooting Ground, where it was fired against a plate to count its spread pattern. At seventy yards the gun provided a reasonably good killing zone of six foot square. Both barrels together fired a total of four hundred and twenty pellets. They fired the gun with a lanyard attached to the trigger, this device removing them from any recoil it might produce; if the gun had been fired untethered, the recoil itself would have been sufficient to launch it into the air.

This photo is captioned on the back in Jack's handwriting:
'Best Day 1964, 219 pigeons Micky Werrell'

Jack's real passion was shooting pigeon. It gave him a combination of fun and country craft that made it a thoroughly satisfying pastime. He made his own hides and his own decoys, one of them a whirling pigeon lure that spun round in the clearing in front of the hide. He also had a particular taste for pigeon and ate it regularly in his youth at Bertorelli's in London. He told the same story, over and over again, about how the birds were being sold in the restaurant for a hundred times what they were worth with feathers on.

Jack's knowledge of guns was evidenced in a letter her wrote to Roy Rich in 1962, which I have no scruples in reproducing here. Roy wanted to deal with the pigeons on his roof and asked Jack for advice.

Dear Roy,

This letter should not be shown to English gun makers.

There is really only one sporting gun worth buying for general purposes and that is a twelve bore. This is the most generally useful gun, giving a pattern of shot about 30 inches across at 35 to 40 yards. This can be varied for a double barrelled gun by choking the mouth of the left hand barrel which then throws this ideal pattern at 40 to 45 yards. The result of this is you can choose which barrel you use according to the range of the target. Incidentally, it is called a twelve bore because if you divide a pound of lead shot into twelve equal parts, a lead ball made from one part will exactly fit the bore. This is a hereditary method of measuring shotgun calibre. There are two other comparatively common sizes of gun; the twenty bore and the sixteen bore but apart from being a bit lighter to carry they have no advantages. A larger gun should not give any greater a recoil because it should be made in proportion to the weight of the shot it fires. The general gun makers' rule is just over 6lbs of gun to 1oz of shot and it will be seen from this that more inertia is automatically provided for each increase in charge and therefore the recoil of all guns should be approximately the same if they are correctly made to suit their cartridges.

Before the war, British guns, particularly what are known as 'best' guns made by the six or seven London makers, were unrivalled anywhere in the world. They were all handmade, they had side locks, they were chopper-lumped and contained many other perfections. It is doubtful whether they shot any better than a good Birmingham gun, but they could be handed down through three or four generations of a family without showing any signs or wear or deterioration. You can still buy such guns from one or two makers. They will now cost you, with purchase tax, anything up to £1,000. And at that you have to be careful because a number of the West End makers now sell Birmingham guns with their own names on them and one at least has his guns made in Belgium.

Therefore, with the exception of the two or three vastly expensive names mentioned above, the difference between English and other guns is now much less. Belgian guns are very reliable. Italian shotguns are now really German shotguns because the Germans made them there during the post-war period when they were forbidden to manufacture arms. Both of these are very good, but a bit clumsy and lacking in balance. However, in recent years we have been importing some Spanish guns. In Spain they still have very skilled gun makers and after about twelve years of apprenticeship they earn about £4 a week. Some enterprising chap has introduced the Spaniards to the type of gun that is required in England and you can now buy them here for about one third of the price of an equivalent English gun. The English gun makers hate them. They have always been rude about foreign guns and they dislike the Spaniards most of all because they are such wonderful value for money.

There is one modern problem in the manufacture of shotguns, which is the alignment of the two barrels. Everything else can now be done by machine methods, but this has to be done by craftsmen who are getting very rare indeed. Consequently, the Americans have developed a single-barrelled repeater, and this has been copied excellently by the Belgians and the Italians. It is not considered a socially acceptable gun in England, though it really only has one disadvantage which is that you can't have two barrels of different chokes. The clay pigeon shooters, who probably now outnumber the game shots, have taken them up enthusiastically and all the champions use them. But you still wouldn't see one at a smart game shoot.

Expensive double-barrelled guns are ejectors, throwing out the empty cartridges as you open the gun. This is quite unnecessary for anything but privileged shooting where the birds come thick and fast. For ordinary rough shooting a non ejector is adequate. The difference in price is anything up to 100%.

If therefore you want a gun just to have a bang at your pigeons, I would buy a good Continental single-barrelled repeater twelve bore; with it you could take up clay pigeon shooting which is a more exhilarating sport. If you think you will be tempted to accept invitations in the shooting field, then you would have to appear with a double-barrelled gun and I personally would buy a good Spanish non-ejector.

If you really want to go no further than getting rid of the pigeons in your garden, then it is my experience that after one good blitz on them they will be wary of the place for a very long time. Therefore, despite this catalogue of information, you should borrow a gun for three or four weeks. I will be delighted to lend you one."

Roy borrowed a gun and successfully dealt with his pigeons, but he never joined Jack in his sport.

As with everything in his life, Jack augmented his love of shooting with a huge amount of knowledge. He knew and understood the reasons why shooting had changed, not only as a sport but how it had changed the countryside itself. He wrote, 'The arrival of Prince Albert, which brought us the first Christmas tree, was also, I fancy, responsible for the first sad turn in the story of the Grey Partridge. From the Schloss estates of his Central European relatives there came to England a new kind of shooting.'

Jack described a new form of shooting where ladies and gentlemen would congregate in great comfort with wine and food and warmth, and a ring of peasants, at a great distance, would walk towards the throng of well-to-do shooters, driving all the game before them. 'There they could be shot,' wrote Jack, 'to the accompaniment of wine-drinking and polite conversation.' The introduction of this Germanic element to the British life did not go unnoticed. Jack said that 'Old Stonehenge' (the English sports writer, John Henry Walsh FRCS of a hundred and fifty years ago) "railed against the importation". He called it the 'Continental Battue'. With hindsight, Jack agreed with Stonehenge that 'the new way would destroy dog work and that was the real pleasure of shooting'. The Continental Battue became Driven Game Shooting and gradually the interaction between dog and man in finding and rising game to be shot did come to an end.

In the centuries before this, the English method of shooting partridge was with three to four sportsmen assisted by what Jack called "wonderfully clever dogs". In the earliest days Setters, having found their game, were trained to point crouched low to the ground so that nets could be drawn over their backs and over a whole covey hidden in the rough.

Later, with the earliest hunting gundogs, they stalked the partridge on his own ground, walking many miles in a day, manoeuvring tactically according to the wind and weather. 'Every outing,' he wrote, 'involved a different set of chess moves, and everyone on the shoot had to understand what he was doing.' He didn't say it, but reading between the lines you can infer that Jack thought this the true origin of the term 'sporting'. He himself thought that a true sportsman was someone who pitted himself against nature, not someone who "simply messed around with a ball in a team on a football field".

Jack pointed out that this was the backbone of English country life, something he thought sadly discarded in Victorian times. Knowing exactly what the country could afford to provide, they never shot too much, and what they did shoot was for their own consumption. "But these were men of patience and moderation. They didn't expect to fill their bags. Four and a half brace would send a man home triumphant." He continued, "It was an art and it all depended on the wonderful dogs, from the best strains of Spanish Pointer, brought back by Wellington's officers from the Peninsular, to some very clever creatures of much less distinction."

However, the Continental Battue took over the sport of shooting and, as such, Jack was not afraid of entering into a class discussion about it. He said, "... the rich were into breech-loading guns with cartridges that gave immediate re-loading. A man could stand square in one place, in line with others of consequence, and have game flown over his head in a continuing aerial salute." Of course, such shooting didn't need dogs other than retrievers, about which Jack quoted Victor Pargeter, calling them "Servants' Hall Dogs! Ought to be wearing a damn apron!"

Modern shoots would take up to five hundred birds in a single day, none of which were for personal use. Instead, they would be hung and sent to markets. Jack did not believe this to be sport but also saw it as the end for the grey partridge. They could not be gathered in sufficient numbers or bred fast enough to fuel this cavalcade of birds put to the gun in comfort. They tried first the red partridge, which was unsuccessfully imported by Charles II, and then they moved on to the pheasant. Modern farming had sprayed away the weeds the grey partridge needed for food and the insects their young needed for nourishment. Stubble was shaved and hay replaced by silage. Thus, everything changed. Jack bemoaned the passing of the old way and the days of the grey partridge.

"Perhaps when some of the modern well-to-do, whose average age is now so much younger, relax sufficiently in their prosperity to cease displaying it and seek again for cultivated ways of doing things. And when the intensity of farming fades and parts of the old landscape we affect to be preserving have a chance to reappear. Perhaps then the voice of the old grey cocks will be heard in the land."

Of course, in order to produce so many birds for shooting, the countryside itself had to change. Jack noted that for the first time the ordinary countryman was not welcome on the land. He would disturb the growing pheasants, and also for the first time, the game keeper became a policeman on behalf of the rich to enforce the separation of the people from the land.

Jack had become the lessee of the Beaulieu Boundary Shoot. This constituted some two thousand acres of land over five farms with woodland, the marshes of the Beaulieu River and the estuary. There were a couple of thousand birds put down each year, fifteen hundred pheasants and a few hundred mallard. There were also a large number of red-legs for shooting. They had eight shares on the shoot, which Jack charged at a fee of £650 in 1975 and this only covered about four fifths of the actual cost of the shoot. Where the rest of the cost came from is not documented, but the sale of dead birds brought in a certain amount. Jack was always concerned to make sure there was plenty of wild stock, and that the land was able to keep the numbers of birds in a wild state without having to over feed or over stock. In this respect he certainly practised what he preached.

Jack's dog, Bess, featured in many episodes of *Country Boy*.

Chapter 11
Jack Speaks Out

Although Jack possessed many cars throughout his life, he came to the conclusion the automobile was the single biggest problem facing mankind. Dr. C. E. M. Joad had said on *The Brains Trust*, a wartime radio programme listened to by several million people, "Man will regret nothing more in his history than the invention of the internal combustion engine." Jack was to use this quotation regularly in his speeches and articles.

In its early days the automobile was little more than an exciting curiosity. During Jack's own childhood they had used the train to get about, and when had joined the Pargeter family at their farm he had used the horse and cart. He told a quaint story about motorists always wanting to use the toilet. In those days toilets were sited outside of the house and, in the countryside, were usually of a type called 'soil middens' where a handful of soil or ash was used to cover the excrement, which was later composted and used on the land. Traditionally the pigeons were kept in the roof space above the toilet and there was often a string pull which hung down into the toilet space to release the birds. Motorists, used to a flushing system, had earned themselves a reputation by releasing the pigeons every time they had finished in the toilet.

Jack said that the economy of the world was over-stretched to carry petrol which fuelled the motor car. The economy of the 1880s was remarkably different from that of the 1930s, but prior to the 1880s it had remained much the same for many generations. From the 1930s onwards the steam train and the horse were being rapidly replaced by the motor car and bus, and the advance of the car was responsible for the disappearance of the traditional boundaries which had existed between town and country.

By the 1960s villages within fifty miles of every major city had become populated by workers commuting to and from that city. The green spaces between the villages themselves were also declining as people's appetites for a desirable rural residence were satiated, so much so that few decent tracts of countryside remained for the purposes of farming or fishing. Hampshire, where Jack lived for many years, was practically vacated in the morning as people travelled to London for work. A steady flow of Londoners who could afford to live fifty miles away from their work were moving into the countryside all around the capital. These people were bringing with them a different attitude to life from those they were replacing in the life of the village.

Their motives for moving were fully understood by Jack, but it was not their motives he questioned, rather the long-term consequences which we could not necessarily anticipate. Even Jack had the benefit of hindsight when making many of his perceptive comments. He wrote, 'It wasn't their fault as such, what else would you expect? But they bring with them the belief that dandelions are supposed to sprout into streetlamps and two acre paddocks were designed to hold twenty eight houses.'

Of course, these people did attempt to integrate into village life, but these attempts were often misjudged, such as the stockbroker complaining of the noise made by the crowing cock or the smell wafting over from the piggery, both of which had been present for generations before the erection of his new architect designed house. And these people were doers and as such they wanted their role on the parish council if only to get the best possible future for 'their' community. Linda Snell from *The Archers* on Radio Four is probably the best-known representation of these interlopers. Their means of integrating was also different; people in the country didn't go in for coffee mornings or cocktail parties, both of which were the rage in London in the forties and fifties. Jack disliked both, calling them, "... a silicon chip method of assembly line hospitality to reach more people than your house was ever meant to contain."

As the migration continued unchecked, people bought up ruined cottages which the farm labourers were all too glad to leave behind. They had them repaired and extended; they installed central heating and new plumbing and increased their value. Planning permission was given for new developments as the newest members on the parish council welcomed more of their own and also because more people meant more rates, which in turn meant more income. Then the farmers began to get rich by selling the land that had stood them in good stead for generations. It was now worth more as a planned housing estate than they would ever earn from it in a lifetime. The decision had been made for them by market forces. Indeed, Simon Baddeley recalls Jack telling him, "Before you die you will be living in the city of England."

He believed there were significant dangers in taking away the ability of the country to feed itself. One day the time would come, he thought, when we would need to feed our own people from our own land, and the prospect of people starving in villages alarmed him. He knew what a hungry city looked like. As a soldier in the war he had found many places which had become cut off from their means of supply. "I can tell you," he once said to a meeting of a Dorset Round Table, "that hungry cities are a frightening sight; a sight I never want to see again." It was only by a supreme effort that we had been able to feed ourselves during the war. In the case of a crisis, we would no longer be able to depend on fruit flown halfway around the world, it would be the continued existence of our own apple orchards which would enable our survival. As petrol became scarce and its price increased, Jack felt that this life would have to change. One of his motives for keeping a pony and trap; he had always had "a feeling that one day the petrol might pack up, and I will be able to continue as we did within a fifteen mile radius when I was a boy."

Jack always had a cart building project on the go.

In his old age Jack sensed a subconscious yearning for a return to a simpler life. "How else could a television programme called *Out of Town* continue for all those years?" he had asked. But that yearning was also combined with a deep anxiety about our ability to sustain the world we had created. Phrases such as "when the oil runs out" were no longer used by the fashionably environmental but appeared from the lips of the masses.

Jack came to believe that governments of all colours simply did not understand the countryside and forced the mentality of the town upon the nation. It was beyond a matter of party politics, it was the inevitable march of a culture that had become separated from the land. The cities controlled the power and wealth of the nation and the countryside was merely one among a number of possible sources for our food.

An economic system called 'Distributism' did hold a certain appeal for Jack. It was characterised by its belief that both capitalism and communism were equally inappropriate for the wellbeing of the environment and the dignity of the population. Instead, it called for the land to be owned by as many people as possible in order to facilitate an agrarian revival. Jack's poem *Grunt of Dissatisfaction* uses the words 'They rule by shuffling papers' which is a direct quote from G. K. Chesterton, one of the leading thinkers of 'Distributism'. The poem is a fine example of the way Jack saw doggerel as a potential weapon among his polite arsenal.

Grunt of Dissatisfaction

It's getting very difficult for us to keep a pig;
The pile of regulations is inordinately big.
Feeding it, moving it, mating it, killing it – everything you try
Is tangled up with red tape, it's enough to make you cry.
I'm sure they'll blame the market but
I'm not sure that it's true;
I think it's our own bureaucrats who fiddle these orders through.
They've never seen a porker and they wouldn't know if they did,
But they've got to keep their jobs up
and they've got to make a quid.
The bureaucratic system is as solid as Stonehenge.
They bitch up all the countryfolk and bugger off home to Penge.
They rule by shuffling papers and the mess that they create
Means the cottage people's pigmeat will soon vanish off the plate.

Now in his mid-seventies, Jack felt the time had come for resistance, a resistance to urbanisation. He felt that something had to be done, and as he said in a number of talks he gave to various Dorset societies, among them the Round Table, The Men of Dorsetshire and the Dorset Agrarian Society, "... who better to call on than the type of people who kept the Saxons out of Dorset, who resisted Cromwell, who but simple farm folk of Dorset."

So what form should this resistance take? For Jack his major weapon was the communication of knowledge about the countryside; he needed to feed this 'unrealised yearning' with information about the way country life should be lived. He became a 'voice in the wilderness'. He talked of New Forest lace makers who had virtually disappeared, calling the last lace makers in the New Forest the "custodians of the art". He talked of the inshore fishermen, now long gone, who used small boats to catch fish using their unique knowledge of the locality. As they had died their knowledge had died with them losing this resource forever. Skills which had been passed on for centuries with no one now left to pass on the great traditions.

He spoke of Larry Skeats who lambed two thousand ewes. He knew every one of them by sight, how they had mothered the previous year and how their mothers had fared before them. It would not be possible to simply 'switch on' the production of sheep as you would turn on a machine; it required an intimate knowledge combined with a real love for the way of life. Larry wrote his own book, *A Shepherd's Delight*, in which he described some of his work with Jack, who had been amazed at the knowledge and skill that Larry had with his sheep. That kind of commitment was not bred or taught in the city.

He also said the knowledge Larry displayed had been handed down from medieval times and was in danger of being lost. Jack had had a sheep which was looking after a young lamb. She had not exactly been rejecting the lamb, but her performance had fallen short. He had sent for Larry who knew exactly what to do. Normally, with lambs about, he would have kept his dog in the Land Rover, but when he saw Jack's duo he brought the dog to the pen. The dog put its paws on the rail which annoyed the sheep, who stamped in response. After just a few moments her protective maternal instincts had been aroused and from that moment on she fulfilled her maternal duties in an exemplary fashion. Without this shepherd's deep and instinctual understanding the lamb would probably have died, yet in times of hardship that very lamb would have meant the difference between plenty and poverty for an entire family.

Jack often said that the greatest way of preserving a thing was to tell people about it. His final years were therefore spent collating as much information as he could about country ways and communicating it to anyone who would listen. His television work had all but ceased, save for an occasional guest appearance, which enabled him to work full time on this project which had become so dear to him.

His resistance was also organised. Politically he had always been mildly conservative. He did not believe in some mythical status quo between land owner and peasant and said that the average countryman was not willing to doff his cap to the landed gentry. More than anything he believed that the logic of a point would win the argument. As such it is no surprise to find that he refrained from anything the viewing public might have perceived as either weird or headstrong; he was not the type to tie himself to a tree or carry a banner, yet he was a formidable enemy.

He had been a founder member of the Anglers Cooperative Association (ACA.) in 1948. Its main focus was, and still is, to fight pollution on behalf of anglers. The association has a string of successes to its credit. They have only lost some three or four court cases over the years and with their team of dedicated lawyers they are prepared to take on businesses, water authorities and farmers alike. The ACA is the only body quoted by anti blood sport campaigners as doing something positive in the field of water conservation. As a member, Jack took on paper mills, cosmetic manufacturers, tar distillers and electroplaters, most of the campaigns meeting with success.

Jack believed that resistance also meant helping others to resist. He was always quick to support his friends in resisting the destruction of the countryside. Phil Drabble was just one who benefited from his subtle support. Phil had been a factory worker from Staffordshire. He had worked hard to become a full time writer and a member of the board of Salters, the company with which he had begun his employment as a youth. Passionate about the countryside, Phil became famous for the television programme *One Man and His Dog*. In the mid-1980s he wrote an angry book in which he pointed the finger at various people who threatened the countryside. Jack wrote the following in a review of the book, *What Price the Countryside?*, in *The Field*.

'... the rhetoric is underlined by an immense knowledge of country life past and present. The outcry may sometimes need earplugs but it is a cry from the heart and never, I think, ill informed. Whatever Drabble is discussing - from the destruction of badgers to the position of tenant farmers or the use of poisons in agriculture - he makes clear the facts behind the argument, and both sides of the argument.'

*

Jack had his own unique way of influencing country matters, yet if you mention his name to the current crop of green campaigners, they may well view him as the opposition. He would hunt, fish and shoot and it is around these activities that new alliances have been formed. But it remains the case that whichever policy might become the saviour of a sustainable way of life in the twenty first century, Jack Hargreaves has probably had a hand in it somewhere. Not only was he well connected and capable of talking to the 'right people', he was also sufficiently motivated by the subject to get himself in front of these people in the first place to make his case.

He argued the case on the Nugent Committee, a powerful group of people gathered together to report on what should be done with all the land the armed forces no longer needed. He was of the view that it should be simply left alone, or returned to its original purpose, in most cases farming. Others argued for public access, public recreation, housing, in fact anything that denied the land its traditional purpose.

Jack at a New Forest drift.

Jack also tried, unsuccessfully, to become a Verderer of the New Forest, a title denoting an overseer of the forest with powers on control over what is permitted, the levying of taxes and how the area is to be preserved. His failure to attain the role is no doubt due to his being very much at odds with the Forest's establishment over issues such as tourism and migration. He viewed it as a considerable snub and in his own polite way showed his anger, not through means of public protest but rather through the use of words in a brief poem called *Forwood Thinking*.

Forwood Thinking

> Verderer, Verderer, where have you been?
> I've been up to London to talk with the Queen
> Of matters so vital they won't stand to mention
> And, having consulted, it's now my intention
> To raise all the prices for pasturing stock.
> I hope this won't come as too much of a shock.

Jack had a working friendship with Julian Huxley, the biologist and broadcaster. The pair debated at length the validity of the 'New Naturalist' both as a series of books by Collins, and as an individual who perceives the countryside in a particular way. Until the arrival of magazines such as *The Countryman*, Jack had viewed nature writing as largely amateur. Huxley was instrumental in the production of the *New Naturalist* series of books which dealt with every topic of British wildlife from moths to badgers. They were new books, looking mostly at individual species or groups and injecting a touch of science into the way people viewed the country. Jack preferred the words of an older generation of natural history writers, written by people themselves close to the country and written for those who wanted a knowledge of the whole rather than its myriad constituent parts.

Jack was of the opinion that the first change in the way man looked at the countryside was forged when nature writing became a mainstream practice. The treatment had become both scientific and educational, designed for a generation which had itself never seen the country at all. Jack was well placed to realise that the natural history genre was the greatest success of post war publishing. The older textbooks were gradually removed, to be replaced each year by a number of new ones complete with maps, statistics and a new way of communicating the wonders of nature.

'Even the phrase 'natural history' became square,' Jack wrote in a review of the *Shire Natural History*. Indeed, the Country Trusts for Natural History had begun to change their names to the County Naturalists' Trusts. It was now true that a person brought up to love the countryside in any traditional sense could find no comfort in a world of societies dedicated to the Victorian notion of the single species. Jack viewed this as a natural consequence of what you fed people; bits rather than the whole, a keyhole glimpse of nature instead of the big picture, a hors d'oeuvre when what you needed was a full and satisfying three course meal. As a further consequence the stewardship of the countryside was also divided up into chunks; some would look after the wellbeing of the birds, others the toads or the voles, but no one looked after the whole thing.

By raising his concerns in debate with people such as Aldous and Julian Huxley, Eric Trist of the Tavistock Institute, Gerald Piel, the editor of *Scientific American*, Sir Peter Scott and academics from a wide range of disciplines and backgrounds, Jack was able to stimulate thought and this mattered a great deal to him.

But it was not his television fame that placed him alongside these people. Some were members of his club, the Savile, where their debates gained something of a reputation. Others he mixed with at the BBC on programmes he either inspired, such as *The Brains Trust*, or those he developed outright such as the *Round Britain Quiz*. He was able to inspire many key people in his own low key but reasoned manner, his impeccable politeness and razor-sharp mind combining to achieve a momentum far more powerful than any raised voices. To some this puts him at odds with the familiar figure who presented *Out of Town*, but Jack the man had been with us for many years before the programme.

The way Jack applied his intellect was certainly not in the least at odds with his role as the presenter of *Out of Town*. Over many years he had built up a picture of humanity and its reaction to change. That change had its roots for Jack in the industrial revolution. As he wrote, 'At the time of the industrial revolution the looms were moved from the cottage lofts down to the mill. From that day on the weaver left his family every time he went to work.' It was a dramatic development for society and one which would certainly leave its mark. Jack strived to understand the way a society could survive this level of change and made a fine job of presenting the evidence.

As the presenter of *Out of Town* he chose to highlight the way of life we were losing in the process, together with its crafts, its sports and its traditions, indeed all the aspects of that disappearing world which Jack himself found so capable of satisfying man's basic hunger. To a large extent he was correct in what were often warnings either of the potential pitfalls, in the case of his 'grown up' television programmes or wonderful time capsules showing us what we risked losing in the case of *Out of Town*, *Country Boy* and *Old Country*. As a veteran of the advertising world perhaps he was simply astute enough to know that the British would never listen to the dour warnings of an intellectual but would gleefully take in the wisdom of a well-loved rural relation complete with his country hat, jacket and omnipresent pipe.

*

Jack was well aware that the world was ruled by the motor car and, despite his hopes to the contrary, the changes it had wrought would be largely permanent. To his deep chagrin the city and the country would never be the same again, and migrants from the city would continue to change the country. He would not ever agree with the idea of the automobile as the greatest liberator. He actually hoped and would have preferred a world without the car regardless of the modern way of thinking about it, and he actively wished that cars would be removed, regardless of the so-called economic consequences. He refused to believe in a world that would continue to be dominated by the motorcar, even if in the future they might just be possibly green in nature.

Jack himself had been the ultimate migrant. Born in London he had spent his early life in the industrial North in middle class comfort. He had then become a copywriter and a broadcaster in the capital, eventually moving to the countryside as financial security permitted yet relying on the city for the bulk of his real income. With more than a little irony, his own life had been the embodiment of everything he was looking to prevent.

In the 1980s Jack had planned to write a book with the working title *A Small Place in the Country* designed to provide information for people thinking of moving from the town to the country. He wanted to help them to understand the culture of the countryside and how to avoid turning it into a tree lined version of the town. Jack was becoming angry, though, that urbanisation had removed even the memory that the town had once itself been the countryside and townsfolk sometimes behaved as though their lifestyle was the only one which mattered. Consequently, he decided he would keep his head down rather than be seen to encourage the migration. The book was never published.

Late in life Jack experienced a feeling of powerless frailty. He was worried about the future we had created, and he had tried to make us aware both of what we were facing and what we were also losing in the process. His stepson Simon Baddeley had been working with a number of respected academics in the late 1980s with a view to exploring many of the issues which concerned Jack and they asked him to record his contribution on tape. It gives us a wonderful opportunity to avoid the pitfalls of assuming what he may have thought. These are his own words transcribed with the permission of his family.

"First of all the condition of the relationship between town and country; there is no doubt that the misunderstanding between the two is worse at the present time than it has ever been in my lifetime and is getting worse still. When I was a very young child, Richard Jeffries wrote that there was nobody in England that was more than two generations from the countryside. In other words, everybody was likely to have at least one granny who still fed the chicken. This was probably true in those days because we were in the very last stages of the migration from country to town which resulted from the industrial revolution.

Cows were still kept in towns; there were still large-scale cow-keepers in Liverpool, I believe, until just before the last war. Market garden crops were grown under the eye of the city. London was supplied with all its vegetables from where Heathrow Airport now stands. Not all that earlier, cattle had still been driven into the London markets on the hoof; in fact, very old country people will still refer to the old blue cattle dogs as Smithfields. Thousands of Eastenders would spend at least a month in the Kent hopfields or in Essex, potato and pea picking. Corn and hay came into the city in huge quantities, because transport was still using horses. People still had a general understanding of animals. In other words, town and country were culturally intermingled.

Now there are two quite separate cultures. A new and entirely urban culture has grown up alongside the older one and the misunderstanding between them is very great. In simplest terms there is a misunderstanding about what the countryside is for. This is at the core of the countryman's relationship with his environment; the countryside is for producing food.

Greater than seven out of ten of the people in England now live in wholly urban surroundings, the majority of them live in large scale conurbations. This same distribution is developing in all other parts of the world; even in the third world. But despite the fact that more than two thirds of the world's population are living in cities, they can only be fed from the countryside. Only the countryside of the world can feed the peoples of the world, apart from the very limited amount that comes from the sea.
Now and again certain wonder cure sources are proposed. I believe that for a number of years Magnus Pike sat in a Glen in Scotland, trying to produce enormous quantities of food yeast that fed on the nitrogen in the

air. But the experiments are said to have come to nothing and I think that this is the time during which he went barmy.

There can be no waste of the countryside to divert it from this primary purpose. Yet in the twenty years during which I have been doing the *Out of Town* programme, the amount of farming land lost to the countryside just about equals the size of the county of Berkshire. Some of the ways in which this loss has been achieved have been very shocking to country people. While I was still working at Agriculture House they were planning the new town of Basingstoke. For years the battle went on to persuade them to take the valueless heaths to the east of Basingstoke for the development. Despite all the pressure they took a very, very large amount of the best agricultural land in the country and populated it with London overspill.

Through modern developments in marketing and retailing, townspeople no longer have a consciousness that all their food has come from the land, so they begin to see the countryside as existing for other purposes of their own. When I served on the Nugent Committee, I found myself opposite John Cripps of the Countryside Commission. I was astounded over the weeks to grasp that, for him, the primary purpose of the countryside was for urban recreation. Over and over again he fought to have large areas set aside for this purpose. "We need large areas for recreation in Nottinghamshire," he would say.

I asked him, at one point, upon what basis rested the assumption that the towns were entitled to use the countryside for recreation? How would it be if I took all the young men in a country village up to London on a Sunday to tear up and down Fitzjohn's Avenue on their motorbikes, and when people complained replied that the countryside needed the town for recreation?

Alas, this idea now seems to be in the mind of townspeople in general. When listening to the radio last summer (1982) I heard a perfectly nice tourist lady, who was staying in a country district, telephone a call-in programme, saying, "I don't understand why farmers are allowed to put fences around their fields and keep people out!" I am sure that it wouldn't surprise her if any other kind of factory were fenced.

The majority of country people have little urge to go to large cities, except for a Christmas shopping expedition, but they are aware that the majority of townspeople seem to want to come to the country. So a new, derogatory name for townspeople has grown up since I was young; they call them 'Grockles'. Some now express the view that townspeople have made the towns unbearable and want to sort out their problems at the expense of the countryside. They cite the summer crowds of 'Grockles' as evidence of this.

The urban mind is not confined to the cities but spreads through the bureaucracy; officials on County Councils are urban minded. Quite recently, people living in an area of farms and villages near where I live were astonished to find their land was designated for future recreational use by Hampshire County Council. Allied to this are some psychological considerations; two separate cultures embrace two separate patterns of attitudes. When you gather large numbers of people together in the same place, the problem with supplying them with services and supplies becomes too difficult to be solved by individuals. It becomes a mass problem involving technology and must be solved centrally by authorities.

Assuming these responsibilities centrally takes away the responsibility of individuals and these things become a matter of entitlement. For example, during the last freeze-up, we heard that people were turning on authority angrily, because they said the streets had not been gritted or salted. People in my district didn't need to say "why didn't they do something about it?" They had already assumed the responsibility of making a way through to at least the nearest main road. A broadcast exhortation to younger people to make sure that the old people were all right was made. Everybody in our village had been seen to by their neighbours by the time this went over the air. This is no judgement of merit between the two sets of attitudes, because they have grown out of their own environments.

In the city you can have complete privacy. You can live in a block of flats with a hundred flats and know only three of your neighbours, but you have no support. Someone could be murdered in the street and people would walk by. There are notorious instances of this. In the country you have no privacy, but you do have great support, right down to the fact that a schoolboy will not only notice that an animal is loose, but he will recognise whose it is and go and report it.

You have to govern your behaviour according to the community that is familiar with you and knows all about you. When I first kept a dinghy on the foreshore down where we lived, if the tide took it away, someone recognised that it was Jack's dinghy and brought it back. Nowadays, the area has been repopulated with newcomers and if you want to keep a dinghy at all you have to fasten it with a lock and chain.

When I was young and visitors came down from the city to the country, we called them hikers in those days. We used to invite them in to tea and sat and listened to them talk about the world they lived in. Nowadays the country people say you must shut your gate and stay inside all weekend because the 'Grockles' are coming. They don't feel comfortable behaving like this. Only two or three years ago (1980), I was fishing with a senior policeman in a country area into which an industrial development had recently been moved. I remember him telling me he had been in the police for thirty-five years and within ten days of people being moved into this enterprise he had known the first theft of a motor car in his career. I am not trying to suggest that country people are totally honest; they have their own, highly developed modes of 'crookery'. It is just another example of the way in which the two cultures are colliding.

Among the ordinary working population of the countryside, one of the biggest sources of resentment is to do with housing. For most of my lifetime people lived near their work, miners in mining villages, farm workers in villages, mill workers in mill towns. The roots of these people went extraordinarily deep. In the Parish of Minstead, for instance, they found the body of William Rufus after his assassination (1100 AD). It was discovered by a forester called Perkiss. He carried it to Winchester with his horse and cart. The Perkiss family have been in Minstead for nearly nine hundred years, and I know a shop worker, a Perkiss, who was born in Minstead Parish within no distance at all from where her ancestor found the body of the King. But there are no Perkisses in Minstead now and there are fewer and fewer New Forest families in the New Forest villages. They all now live in the surrounding developments, in council houses, their cottages having been taken over by the middle classes, in particular by the business bourgeoisie.

The man who works for me, Reg Cole, a member of an old local family, now lives on a housing estate in Pennington. He expresses his pleasure at being in the Forest instead of being at home where he lives. Those cottages in range of my house which in the past have always been occupied by farm workers are now lived in respectively by an accountant, a lawyer from Southampton, the clerk of the courts from Winchester, an antique dealer, a Cypriot chain caterer, a marketing man and a distributor of 'French Letters'.

It is the motor car that has enabled these people to live in these houses and none of them could get to work in a petrol strike. In the one remaining cottage opposite me lives a ninety-year-old man; he was listed in the 1910 Kelly's Directory as one of the small farmers of the parish. Everybody knows that when he dies the cottage will be worth such a lot of money, even unconverted, that there is virtually no chance of a countryman living in it. Cottagers would find it impossible to raise the money to complete the repairs to these cottages to bring them up to modern standards. It is not just territorialism, but country people become irate when these cottages are inhabited as second homes. Communities are broken up and the totally acquainted, mutually supporting community fails, because the new people do not naturally have the country way in their blood. Consequently, when villages become dormitories, local schools are closed because there are no longer children to populate them.

Our local publican, last summer, when the weather was hot and townspeople were here in very large numbers at the weekends, and there was a strike of draymen interrupting supplies to the pub, decided that he was going to keep his beer for his regular customers, whose club the pub was all year round. He suffered anger from visitors who felt they were entitled to buy his beer.

Is the country one extended suburb on which townspeople can call for relief? Of course, scale is relevant. It is a fact, taking Hampshire as an example; the weekend motoring visitors to the countryside have been increasing at a rate of 20% annually. It is in such circumstances that things that were once acceptable become intolerable. It has been said and accepted that visitors have been good for trade. This argument was propagated by small local councils which were made up very largely of tradespeople. It used to be said that a meeting of the council and the board of trade could be changed merely by changing the agenda. Ironically, when smaller councils have less power, a wider variety of people are going for council membership and new arguments are being heard.

In the West Country, and also more widely, people are starting to say "we don't want tourists, they clutter up the place". The jobs are only for the summer; they are no good in the winter. What we want is local industry, sited in the right place, so that those people that can't be employed in the country can get jobs all the year round. This is, of course, a return to earlier things. In the past there were always industries for those on the farms who were surplus to the needs of the farm. Where I come from, in the West Riding of Yorkshire, you always had brothers and uncles who were in the mines or in the mills, even though you all lived on the farm. It is certainly true that village traders are no longer a family part of the community as they used to be, many of them come in from elsewhere and many of the shops are devoted entirely to Grockles. I know villages with two antique shops and four gift shops out of a total of ten or twelve businesses.

Country people do not understand the union state mind of the 'townie'. When, in recent bad weather, airport workers were refusing to stand on frozen snow in order to get aeroplanes ready on the tarmac, shepherds were up to their waists in snow caring for their flocks. When the dustmen claimed the roads were impassable, the milk lorries managed to get through every day. The NFU has never had a strike, though it has had some very tough pay negotiations. Some people say their union leaders can't call all their men together for a show of hands meeting. The fact is the attitude to the job is different, and the attitude of workers to employers is different. The minimum wage is very low and greatly advertised as such, and that is because there is a large section of family farms who can afford to keep no more than one man and still not pay him very well. But you can take it as true that within the substantial part of the industry, you will find it very difficult to find a man who is earning the union minimum. Most of them are earning considerably more.

The issue of tied houses has been an article of faith of the socialist party in that they will get rid of tied housing in agriculture, but country people wonder why it is right to have tied housing in the police, fire brigade, water supply companies and teaching, but not agriculture. They also know it is very difficult to get labour without a cottage.

Another subject that shows root differences in attitudes is that of public footpaths. Country people know and farmers will tell you that footpaths were built for working reasons. When people went to work in various fields they took certain routes that were customary ways that had a work-a-day purpose. Now they are claimed by outsiders for recreational reasons. It is appallingly difficult to get an alternative route accepted when it is altered. There is a row going on about farmers putting bulls in fields where there is a public footpath. It reveals what is actually behind this subject. There are farms which happen to be placed close to villages which have public footpaths on more than 50% of their fields. If a farmer is a breeder of beef cattle he wants to turn his bull out with his herd for several months of the year. If he is rotating his crops, as he should, there are seasons where it is impossible for him to put his bull with his cows without putting them near a public footpath. This argument has got hotter and it has been decided that a farmer can put his bull in any field as long as the farmer gives proper notice. The Ramblers Association is furious about it. As I said, the footpaths were customary ways and in general, people in the countryside walked where they liked because they were known, and they could get at your family if you got up mischief.

It was only in Victorian times that the country people were excluded from large areas and game keepers started to push people around. Again, a famous country writer from my youth, W.H. Hudson, was still saying that it was the wretched continental practice of driven game shooting which had excluded the countryman from his usual pattern of walking across the countryside and made customary ways more important. This has led to the fact that the sport of shooting has become an urban one. It is so expensive and has such a social flavour to it that now the guns on the larger shoots are paid for at anything from £650 to £1500 per year, largely by business executives. It is very difficult for an ordinary countryman to get a bit of shooting.

I can remember when the first Birmingham man came down to fish the Hampshire Avon. Nowadays the big fishing associations are taking over the fishing, with very large funds. More and more fishing associations are being pushed out. The Newbury Anglers, a hundred year old fishing association, tried to get the fishing on the River Kennett when it became free, but the London Transport Fishing Association came along with a great deal of money at their disposal, and free buses at the weekend to bring them down, and took it over at a price which the local club had no chance of meeting. On many of our rivers a local chap has to get up very early to get a spot on a river. It is the motor car and the motor coach that has allowed this. When I was young, a man fished as far away as he could get on a bicycle. If you ask the Birmingham Anglers, one of the most powerful organisations in England, you will find they have waters as far away as the middle of Lincolnshire and their annual motor coach bill will run into tens of thousands of pounds a year.

For these and allied reasons the countryman believes he is living in occupied country. Not least because the tax and capital management has resulted in the country and agricultural land becoming an investment. The arrival of large institutions as owners of great stretches of countryside is a major problem. In many cases they don't even care what they do with it. I was asked by a local agent if I wanted to buy the lease on small farm that was close to my own farm. I asked who had bought the farm; he wouldn't tell me, but when I asked what they would do with the land he replied: "Do with it? They're not even going to look at it for the next twenty years!" The countryman asks if it is wrong for investors to have large numbers of urban dwellings as a plaything, why they should be allowed to do the same with the countryside.

Politics is a hotbed of debate in the countryside. Huge amounts of rate support grant (in the early 1980s) is being removed from the country areas and transferred to the cities. The government said this was because the cities have desperate problems. Socialists believe that the countryside is irretrievably lost to the conservatives, and again this is a misunderstanding of the real truth. They believe that country people naturally defer to the upper classes. In fact they don't like them or respect them any more than any other part of the working population does; the attitude can be misunderstood because of the total acquaintanceship of the country. Being on first name terms with a Lord doesn't mean you automatically defer to him in any way. Labour governments since the rise of Mr Wilson have not understood the country things and country people have had no sympathy with them. But Tom Williams, who became Labour Minister of Agriculture in 1945, was for many years the darling of the countryside and is believed to know more about the problems than any new minister since. From this time on Labour could have won the countryside. My father was a socialist and he and his friends bought *The Clarion* every week and read what Robert Blatchford had to say about the socialist country policy; they would feel very let down nowadays. This short order cooking of contemporary Parliamentary democracy cannot serve the countryside well.

I remember an industrialist who took up farming as an occupation, who said to me that he was absolutely astounded and shocked by the idea that it took you three years to turn over your money. It does in fact take three years to produce a beef steak and sometimes the animal can be worth less two years after you started on it. Three years ago, at the time of the drought, infant cattle were worth about fifty bob (£2.50). This didn't cover the cost of transporting them to market. Today exactly similar animals are worth £100. Imagine any industrial organisation coping with that! They would think they were living in a mad world. It needs an entirely different set of assumptions to cope with country production. But when you realise the amount of imported foodstuffs it makes you wonder what the government thinks is the actual nature of British farming.

Farming today depends on a huge amount of mineral oils, and although it is vaulted as the most efficient in the world this efficiency is measured simply in financial terms. I don't know the actual figure for how much energy is needed to produce one unit of energy in terms of food, but it is frightening; something in the nature of a thousand to one, whereas it is thirty to one in the peasant farming of China. If oil is to become unavailable, then it is possible that only those people skilled in small scale subsistence farming will be able to keep anyone alive. Those farming communities which are being more and more pushed into obsolescence may in fact be the world's most vital resource.

For me all the foregoing leads to one question: whether the old agrarian culture is to be deemed out of date, to be completely overtaken by the urban industrial one. It is happening now. Should it be allowed to happen or should it be thought about?"

*

One of Jack's doggerel poems dealt with 'Grockles' and their impact:

The Great Invasion

The purple shouting groccoli
Are sprouting everywhere.
The foresters are furious,
The council doesn't care.
The tradesmen are delighted
And the giftshops clear their stocks.
The pubs have all been altered
So their image suits the grocks.
The Forestry Commission
Says there's no need for alarm.
"The Forest's getting wilder".
(They expect it to keep calm?)
It's time that we considered
Just how long this trend can last
For the purple shouting groccoli
Are multiplying fast.

Chapter 12
Whatever Happened to Jack?

A question often put to Fred Dinenage was "Whatever happened to Jack?" and in the *Portsmouth News* in 1992 he got Jack to respond. Of course, Jack was still going strong then. "I grow all my own food, I drive my pony and trap, and I feel as good as I did when I was sixty," he said. His old grandfather had told him that if he drank cider and ate honey every day, he would live to be ninety. Jack was still only eighty-one and his grandfather's recipe for longevity was serving him well. He went on to add, "My grandfather lived until he was ninety-one, and then they say he drank himself to death."

Jack had an army of pipes and although it was rumoured he grew his own tobacco, no reference was ever made to it by him except on a tape he was making about the changes to the countryside. He said that Polish immigrant farmers in Wales after the First World War grew their own tobacco for themselves and their friends and got themselves into trouble with the police as a result.

Jack was still regularly fishing on the River Allen despite its reduced flow, but he was not strong enough to go to sea as much as he once had. Fishing the various waters he had known so well in former years had all but come to an end. He offered all his sea fishing equipment for sale for the benefit of the Dorset Trust for Nature Conservation. There were more than a dozen excellent sea fishing outfits for everything from flounders to wreck-fish and big skate, together with reels and tackle. The proceeds, some £565, were sent to the Trust, everything scooped up by an eager public thrilled to be buying Jack's kit. Among them was an outboard engine which brought in less cash than some of his rods and reels.

Jack was aware that his life was less than exemplary, certainly with regard to his family, but in his eighties he took to setting things right. He spent considerably more time with Simon. On Jack's birthday on New Year's Eve of 1991 they spent the day deep in conversation about his father's war time record, his mother's relationship with Jack and how, in the end, Jack looked back to be very grateful for his time with her. Many ghosts were put to rest, but others remained. Jack had heard no words form his second family in his old age, and although his first family had been in touch, their approaches had been politely diverted away.

*

Jack attended a reunion show for Southern Television called *Southern Gold* early in 1994 and confessed that it would probably be his last television appearance. He knew he was unwell but had hardly consulted either the hospital or his doctor. He had cancer and was in fact very ill. Right up until his last few days when he became very unwell, Jack was functioning as normal. He had done his rounds that day according to his regular public house routine which he had followed almost every day of his last few years.

Jack had been no stranger to the occasional migraine headache, and he had usually needed to take a day off to recover. When he fell ill with a severe headache he simply assumed it would be another one of those days, but he was wrong. He entered hospital at the end of the first week in March and Isobel, aware of his rapid deterioration, telephoned the family.

Jack slept for much of the time in his room at the hospital overlooking the Dorchester fields. Isobel had placed spring flowers by the bed and the room was busy with the coming and going of concerned friends and relatives. Bay told everyone of a dream she had had of rivers full of fish, inspired, no doubt, by Jack's fondness for fishing.

*

Simon was worried what he would find when he visited Jack in hospital; he registered his concern in his diary. Would Jack be embarrassed? Maybe he would feel that there were things which needed to be said at this late stage in his life. In fact Jack was unconscious and unable to communicate. Was he dreaming and if so where were the dreams taking him? If he was still aware of his long and eventful life, would he be trying to communicate and if he did wish to say something, what would his message be?

*

Isobel was clearly finding it difficult to cope. She had always been at her most comfortable when in control of a situation but now she could not protect Jack as she had done so for many years. Her usual strengths now only served to emphasis her present helplessness. For no reason other than perhaps the instinct of a woman reflecting on what might have been done better, she told Simon and Bay that Jack had had his fair share of problems with women in the past and that this history had drifted into her relationship with both Simon and Bay. There were tears, but Simon managed to put them all at ease: "He might have had some problems with women, but not for the last thirty years," he said, and together with a tearful hug it was all that was needed to be said.

It was difficult to imagine what was going on in Jack's mind for those looking on. How was he at that moment? Where were his thoughts now? Was he dreaming and if so were there regrets about the past or was he simply off fishing somewhere in Bay's dream? No one would ever know, and that's exactly as Jack probably would have wanted it.

Jack spent the last three days of his life in a coma. He died at eight o'clock on the evening on the fifteenth of March in 1994. His family rushed to Dorchester to be with both him and Isobel. As perhaps a fitting tribute that same evening saw the broadcast of Jack's final television appearance, the Southern Television reunion where Jack said his goodbyes to a fond public. The show's broadcast that evening had been pure coincidence, but somehow it had seemed so right. The cause of death was a tumour in the throat.

Throughout his life Jack consistently warned against the 'ides of March', strange for a logical, un-superstitious person. The word 'ides' comes from the Latin, translated as 'to divide'; they were simply the middle of the month and for most months this meant the fifteenth. Julius Caesar was told to beware them, for good reason, and so did Jack. For most of his life Jack would say with some meaning, "Beware the ides of March." It was one of those constant features that people never actually took any notice of. But Jack died on the ides of March.

*

Many eulogies followed Jack's death. *The Times* wrote that he took with him 'a love of traditional life that did much to enhance to viewers appreciation of country ways'. Many more kind words were to follow from people who knew him, but most of all from people who felt they had known him.

The funeral took place the following week. There were no crowds, just family and friends. After the singing of hymns, Simon read the poem *Afterwards* by Thomas Hardy:

Afterwards

'When the present has latched its postern behind my tremulous stay,
And the May month flaps its glad green wings like leaves,
Delicate-filmed and new-spun silk, will the neighbours say,
"He was a man who used to notice such things?"

If it be in the dusk when, like an eyelid's soundless blink,
The dewfall-hawk comes when crossing the shades to alight
Upon the wind-warped upland thorn, a gazer may think,
"To him this must have been a familiar sight."

If I pass during some nocturnal blackness, mothy and warm,
When the hedgehog travels furtively over the lawn,
One may say, "He strove that such innocent creatures should come to no harm,
But he could do little for them; and now he is gone."

If, when hearing that I have been stilled at last, they stand at the door,
Watching the full-starred heavens that winter sees,
Will this thought rise on those who will meet my face no more,
"He was one who had an eye for such mysteries?"

And will any say when my bell of quittance is heard in the gloom,
And a crossing breeze cuts a pause in its outrollings,
Till they rise again, as they were a new bell's boom,
"He hears it not now, but used to notice such things?"

It seemed to sum up Jack and his hopes. He had also been very fond of the works of Thomas Hardy.

Andrew Richards, the minister, recalled that a lady had once come up to Jack and asked, "Didn't you used to be Jack Hargreaves?" "I think so!" he replied. The congregation smiled as they recalled Jack's dry wit, and that was how the minister chose to remember him. He described Jack was a witty and articulate renaissance man, a man who loved and was greatly loved in return.

Isobel's status as Jack's widow was not in question, but this did not come at the expense of his earlier relationship with Barbara, at least not in Bay's mind. She certainly disagreed with any suggestion that he had been happier with Isobel than with Barbara but only mentioned this to Simon.

It was more than just loyalty to her mother; it was the memories of those great and happy times they had all shared together as a family, and what was the role of a funeral if not remembrance?

The memorial service was attended by only a select few. Bernard Venables, described as the best angling writer of the twentieth century, spoke of the warm days he had spent with Jack, fishing, filming or illustrating Jack's book, *Fishing for a Year*. While Jack had been writing the book, Bernard had been preparing the best-selling angling book of all time, *Mr Crabtree Goes Fishing*. This book, an illustrated guide to fishing, gave Jack and Bernard an idea for a cartoon strip about a detective. Jack had tried without success to sell the idea to the national newspapers.

Jack's old friend and colleague, Cliff Mitchelmore, read a chapter from Jack's book, *The Old Country*. "The May Dance that was happening in the sun that day was first made up of a mob of fluttering females, all ready for what can happen as a result of going to dances." It seemed to reflect something of the twinkle in Jack's eyes.

George Egan also spoke warmly of Jack and many days spent filming wonderful programmes. He told of how Jack had been totally unflappable and how he could literally "talk for England." He believed Jack to be a true genius, someone who came along just once in a lifetime, and George had been privileged to work with him for many years. Phil Dace of the Out of Town Centre also spoke of Jack's vision to give children an opportunity to see cows milked and hens lay eggs, and he thanked Jack on behalf of the thousands of children who had stayed at the centre. Jack Reece talked about the debt sea anglers owed to Jack, in particular the Southern Television Fishing Trophy.

As the service came to an end the *Out of Town* theme tune was played.

Real life resumed again in the hotel after the service. Muffled voices and polite conversations filled the room. All that was missing was Jack. Isobel, now so much more vulnerable than in former years, engaged people in conversation. With no Jack to shield from the outside world, her protective instincts could relax a little and, for the first time in thirty years, she stepped forward to openly welcome Jack's wider family, now all united by a common grief.

Raven Cottage was quiet. It had often been quiet, but this was a different and uncertain silence. The clocks which had ticked away the time before

Jack's return from filming, work or the shed, now simply went on ticking. Letters and visits from friends amused her and helped to pass the time, but they never filled the void left by Jack. She was unable to watch Jack's final broadcast from the night of his death, although she did have the tape. Clearing out Jack's shed and filing his remaining papers was a very painful process, but she felt it would perhaps prepare her for the inevitable sadness of future tributes and anniversaries to come. Her final act of respect was to scatter his ashes over the side of the hill on Bullbarrow which overlooked Belchalwell where he had lived for many years. It had been the same place where Tess Durbyfield had ridden her father's horse, Prince, into the mail coach. It had died, pierced by a shaft of wood, in Jack's favourite novel, *Tess of the Durbervilles* by Thomas Hardy.

Isobel made a living will and became a member of the Voluntary Euthanasia Society. She passed away in 1998. Simon Baddeley and Jack's old friend Len Smith scattered her ashes on Bullbarrow Hill where three years earlier she had done the same for Jack. As they did so, Len, ever the Gypsy romantic, spotted two kestrels rising together. He believed Jack and Isobel were together again.

Chapter 13
Jack's Mail Bag

Reading Jack's mail now, twelve years after his death, has been something of a humbling affair. Each communication had been carefully dated on receipt, then answered and finally referenced by Isobel, ever the perfect personal assistant. The letters discuss fond memories of the countryside and how his programmes helped either to recall some lost thoughts of it or, indeed, even helped nurture their early interest in it. They came from townsfolk and country dwellers alike and from people of all ages. His weekly programmes seemed to inspire both admiration and curiosity in equal measure.

Often people would write for information. The questions ranged from the theme music and where could they get a copy, to 'where is the best place to catch a certain kind of fish?' or 'what was the name of that animal you showed three weeks ago?' They were all replied to on a postcard. At other times he would be asked where he usually fished so they could have a picnic together, or which pub he liked the most so they could buy him a pint. Others were more personal, such as the one from a lady of eighty who signed herself 'An Admirer Indeed', and wrote, 'You may be no Mohammed Ali but for me you're the greatest!'

One consistent fact was that people felt they knew him personally. Many asked if they could address him as Jack; after all, he did appear in their living room every week and was always welcomed. A gentleman telephoned Jack to ask if he wanted to fish on his river. Ever excited at the prospect of new waters Jack asked the gentleman's name. He was hurt by the question. He knew Jack's name so why didn't Jack know his? The new medium of television seemed at times to confuse. One woman wrote to Jack with the following question. 'I watch your programme every week, it is delightful! By the way, how do you like my new curtains?' Jack's response is not recorded.

Jack's easy style was measured and calculated. He could have done *Out of Town* in a dinner suit; he had several and was certainly no stranger to wearing them, but he chose to wear a different costume, one appropriate to the subject matter. This was due in part to the fact that *Out of Town* evolved out of *Gone Fishing*, and Jack had to wear fishing clothes for that show. But he also felt comfortable in the clothes he wore for *Out of Town*. His pipe, his hat and the warmth of his manner endeared him to people. He was also wise enough to know that nobody would have taken him seriously had he spoken to his public from a shed whilst wearing a dinner suit!

In the earliest days of the *Out of Town* series there were many viewers who were grateful for his having brought back memories of their youth. It was avidly watched by people who had once lived either on a farm or in a village, but no longer did so, and they were appreciative of Jack having shown them again what they had known all those years ago. It reassured them to hear Jack saying how important these things were and how he hoped they would remain a part of everyday life as they often had for hundreds of years.

Many people chose to tell Jack of things they remembered from their youth. Letters such as, 'We had a cart just like yours on last week's show ...' were commonplace and were usually answered with a letter which detailed some interesting point or other about Jack's own cart. As a general rule, his responses were kept to a similar length to the original communication.

One viewer thought that Jack had not invented *Out of Town*. 'We have watched your programme since you took over from dear Ollie Kite.' Ollie was a fishing presenter on Southern Television and a naturalist who had made all sorts of programmes for the network, but Jack had not followed on from him, indeed they had often broadcast together, and Ollie had enjoyed a regular role as a special uncle on *Country Boy*.

In 1965 a viewer wrote to thank Jack for his tribute to Winston Churchill in *Out of Town* on the death of the great leader. 'As an ex-Desert Rat and Paratrooper, who has seen some bull put on for the big nobs, I can imagine Winnie chuckling to himself. Thank you, Jack for a proper ex-serviceman's tribute.' Jack thanked him and commented that he had met Winston on a couple of occasions, both in the Tank Regiment and when working on special advertising projects for the Conservative Party.

Jack received many photographs and pictures in the mail. One was a newspaper clipping along with a letter which said, 'We think our son may be your youngest fan, is he? We hope you don't mind but we took the liberty of entering him into the local carnival as 'Jack Hargreaves of Out of Town' with pipe and all!' The child, dressed in fishing hat and sporting a pipe, won third prize. Jack replied that he thought he was better looking than the original.

Jack had once made a film for *Out of Town* where he took a gentleman who was over one hundred years of age fishing. It was his birthday and he had always fished a particular river. The old gentleman, G. J. Dunton, was carried out to the riverbank to fish. His daughter wrote to thank Jack for his kindness on her father's behalf saying, '... he always intended to write himself but he kept falling asleep!'

As if he didn't have enough problems with women, many of his letters were from ladies of a certain age, some who seemed to fancy their chances with him; one such letter describes a lady who 'can carry a voice in my head, so that your delightfully clear English voice will remain with me always.' Another wrote to complain. She had been telling her friends at work about her first television set. All that was on was 'an old chap talking about fishing.' Her friends were amazed. One said, "What? That's Jack Hargreaves! My husband wouldn't miss him for the world!"

At the end of Jack's career he received many letters from people expressing their sadness as they realised he had broadcast his last programme. One wrote, 'I was saddened when I realised that it was the last time you were going to pop into my living room for a chat.' Another wrote, 'When you raised your glass and said farewell it left me feeling numb. I wanted to say 'Good bye' to an old friend.'

One viewer went further, writing, 'to me your manner had the charm of a Dave Allen, a Bob Hope, a Grapelli, a Paul Daniels and those others who don't have to work at it to look good.' The most militant correspondent urged action and wrote a threatening letter to the Director of Programme with the words, 'I am about to organise a mammoth protest march and demonstration outside the ITA Headquarters, Downing Street, Lambeth Palace and the LSE to demand the immediate return of Jack Hargreaves. PS And I won't be put off with a paltry fifteen minutes on a Friday either!'

Among Jack's letters kept after his death by Isobel, is a large pile labelled 'Yes.' A smaller pile is labelled 'No' and an even smaller one bears simply a question mark. These all refer to various requests for Jack to make a public appearance. The 'Yes' pile includes gardening clubs, rotary clubs, a fivepenny club, a school talk on conservation, a dinner dance (which he would have hated), the 75th anniversary of the Romsey NFU, various church fêtes, a discussion club, a talk at the fly dressers' club, a number of hunt dinners, a dinner of the Society of Dorset Men and umpteen county fairs.

The 'No' list included the third Dorset Literature Festival, a Young Farmers event in Dorchester, the Dorset World Wildlife Fund, the Tarrant, Gunville and Hinton Conservatives and a number which he could not have managed due to other commitments including a Radio Lancashire chat show in memory of his old friend Dick Walker.

One letter which had not been expected had arrived in 1972. Jack had been working on the Nugent Committee, set up to discuss how ex-military land would be best put to use. The following letter appeared at the end of the period of office.

```
Sir,

The Prime Minister has asked me to inform you, in
strict confidence, that he has it in mind, on the
occasion of the forthcoming list of New Year
Honours, to submit your name to the Queen with a
recommendation that Her Majesty may be graciously
pleased to approve that you be appointed an Officer
of the Order of the British Empire (OBE).

Before doing so, the Prime Minister would be glad
to be assured that this would be agreeable to you.
I should be grateful if you would let me know by
completing the enclosed form and sending it to me
by return of post.
```

Jack was pleased to receive this award, but he knew that it was for his having sat on the Nugent Committee and not for services to television. He joked privately that the honour was not sufficiently high for him to refuse it with dignity, but he was delighted to receive it. He was inundated with congratulatory letters from well wishers. His friend and solicitor, Mike Brown, was just one of them. His son apparently said that "it was worth being bitten by a donkey to have the honour of knowing Jack!" It had in fact happened to one of them on a visit.

Jack replied, "As a matter of fact, to have your 60th birthday, do the 500th *Out of Town* and get your OBE all in twenty four hours is the kind of turn up of the odds which, in other circumstance, would have won me the pools. Still, I'd swap the lot for not being sixty!"

Jack received a lot of mail from fellow members of the Order. Harry Fowler, the actor, sent a merry 'Welcome to the Club!', as did Marjorie Proops, the agony aunt. She signed her letter 'Margeobe' and Jack replied to her that he thought they made a good pair! Alastair Burnett, then Editor of *The Economist* and later a television news reader, wrote to say that from that time on they would all have to treat Jack with even more respect. Jack replied that now he lived 'as a yokel - it is *The Economist* that makes me feel in touch with world.'

It was letters, though, from people who had something of an insight into Jack's old world which touched him most. Amy Gentry OBE, Captain of the Weybridge Ladies' Amateur Rowing Club, had a great love for the country, and the experiences of a long life in it. She wrote, telling of her raising a lost cygnet to adulthood and of numerous ducklings she had reared. Her father, Major Gentry, was a great friend of Oliver Pike, who was in turn a great friend of Jack's. She also told him of her first ever nature moving picture, *Pike's Life Cycle of the Great Crested Grebe*. She ended her letter with a post script; 'What pleasure there is all around us if only people had the eyes to see it.'

One particular viewer wrote nostalgically to say that he remembered a fishing holiday in 1900, when he was four years old. He recalled, in particular, this holiday to Bournemouth, because at Waterloo Station he watched the train loads of soldiers going off to the Boer War. His story went on, 'After the First World War, I married and came to live at Swaythling, surrounded by fields and two delightful lakes. Monks Brook was teeming with trout (and is now so polluted that not even eels live there). Alas, during the last fifteen years the Green Belt in front of my house has been built upon, and if I want to live 'out of town' I shall have to move further out again. But I feel too old for that now.' 'It seems to me,' replied Jack, 'that your attitude to life is much the same as my own and that you are pretty good at enjoying yourself. May you do so for a long time to come.'

Perhaps the most touching 'little note' came from Jack's aunt Edith. It was her husband, Stanley, who had taught Jack to fish all those years ago.

Edith wrote:

```
Dear Jack,

Congratulations on your having been awarded the OBE.
Well done, you deserve it! Your programmes have been
the most interesting of any.

Stanley never missed one if he could help it. In
addition to all the other work you have done for I.T.V.
programmes, how proud your father would be if only he
had been alive now. Best love and further success in
your career.
```

There were also letters and parcels which had provided Jack with some kind of gift or other. A viewer from Cheadle in Cheshire wrote to Jack to say, 'I have enclosed a limited print of my drawings (of fishing scenes) which I hope you will accept with my compliments in the hope that it will give you a little pleasure in return for the endless pleasure you have given me. Many thanks.'

He also received many jars of preserves, various items of produce, tied fish flies, horse hair, horseshoes, photographs of animals, children, cakes and the odd dead animal to identify.

The fan mail did not stop coming after Jack's death. Isobel tried to answer many of the letters, though some were so touching that she found it difficult. The most distressing were those, who, unaware of Jack's death, wrote to ask how he was doing and when would they be able to see him on the screen again. She simply felt she could not disappoint them and found herself unable to respond, if only for reasons of compassion. She only ignored one other kind of letter; those from the souvenir hunters. Various pubs wrote to find out if they could have various items in memory of Jack, but all too often all they wanted was to display something of his in the bar.

Jack's letters revealed a man adored by his public, both young and old alike, and for a period of over thirty years. Apart from the odd, 'I don't think that you got it quite right, Mr Hargreaves,' virtually every one of the thousands of letters that landed in his post bag was complimentary. I am sure it goes without saying that many people will still retain and treasure the responses they received back from him.

It is appropriate that Jack be given the final word:

Ode to a book I never wrote

Did they think about the skylarks
When they built Mayfair
on the grazings that ran down
to the Shepherd's Market?

Did they worry about the snipe
when they drained the marshes
behind St. James's Palace
to build Belgravia?

Where did the kite go
when they dug the London sewers?
Do the piles they drove down
through the beaver's dam
hold firm the supermarket
in Newbury High Street?

Who cooked the big trout
that lay under the village bridge at Wandsworth?
Who feasted on the last salmon
that was netted at Tower Hamlets?

Now they come to put central heating
in the ploughman's hovel.
They claim the sun that used to bake the hay,
And breathe the breeze in which the pointing dog
caught a hundred scents.

They walk out in trainers
and T-shirts that say, 'Save the Rain Forest'.
"Stand back!" they say.
"We have a right to walk where we please!"
But we look where they trod before
and shudder for what follows in their footsteps.

I said I must write a warning.
But I was angry and – as the
Japanese say – to be angry
is only to make yourself ridiculous.
So we will live out our days
in the cracks between the concrete.
And then they will pour cement on top of us.

How *Out of Town* and *Old Country* were produced
by Dave Knowles

I worked on *Out of Town* for many years as the editor at Southern Television, and I then produced all of the *Old Country* programmes for Channel 4.

At Southern Television all *Out of Town* programmes were shot on 16mm film with no sound. When the film arrived in the cutting room, I would sit with Jack and go through the rushes. He would tell me the story he wanted to tell and the length he wanted to end up with. This was usually around ten minutes as we normally had one film in the first half of the programme and one in the second. I would then edit the programme and call him back to look at it and approve it. Because of our very close working relationship, I normally knew exactly what he wanted to show, so changes were very rare.

Once Jack had seen the film, I laid the sound track by finding effects to cover what was happening in the pictures. When I had laid the sound track, I took it into the sound department and we mixed all the tracks together. At Southern Television it was common practice to transfer the sound onto the sound stripe that ran down the edge of the 16mm film. Generally in television, film was broadcast with the sound coming from a separate track, which was the same size as 16mm film but had a magnetic coating, but at Southern they did not like doing this as it was thought that if either the telecine or sound machine had a problem then the sound would be lost.

The downside of this was, however, that the sound quality was nowhere near as good from the stripe, because the area was much smaller and the film had joins which tended to cause bumps as they went over the sound heads. One thing you do need to remember is that the sound coming out of a television at that time cut off all the highs, so the overall quality was always pretty low.

While on the subject of quality, it should also be remembered that 16mm reversal film was not good. In fact, when video first became popular with the advent of U-Matic it was considered far superior to film, although it had a resolution far below that of an early basic mobile phone camera.

The *Out of Town* edited stories went into the studio on a Monday morning and everything had to be ready by 9:30 am. On our arrival at Southern, we were given a running order for the film inserts for the programme. Let's say the two films were fly fishing in the first half and donkey racing in the second - these had to be made up onto spools and got down to telecine (which was at the other end of the building) by 9:30. If you ever get a chance to look at one of the programmes that went out, you would see little dots in the top right hand of the film that appear 3 seconds before the end. These we had to add to let the production crew know when the film was going to run out, so that they could be ready to mix back to the studio sections.

After we had got the film down to telecine, everything was out of the editor's hands, and George Egan, the studio director, took over. For *Out of Town* they used the smallest studio, which I think was studio 3. This studio was also used for *Day by Day* so Jack's set (his famous shed) had to be set up in the morning. Jack would bring in whatever props (maybe fishing rods, horse harness) he needed for that morning's recording. They would then do a run through of the complete programme, which was unscripted. Jack would sit on his stool with a little monitor in front of him (out of shot) on which he could watch the film inserts and just talk for their duration. He was never worried about making a small error in information as he always said to me that this created viewer participation.

After the run through, which finished around 10:15, they then went for the recording, which, as with the rehearsal, was ad-libbed by Jack. I can only remember one occasion when he asked for a retake. The titles for the programmes, with the title music, were fed in from tape and everything was conducted like a live broadcast.

A dear friend of mine to this day is John Ryder who worked in the Design Department at Southern Television. John remembers popping into the studio one day when *Out of Town* was being recorded. The tea break had been called and he expected to find an abandoned studio, the crew having 'dropped all tools' to rush off to the canteen for a cup of tea and a bun. But all hands were still there, and at the centre was Jack, telling one of his stories. Such was the spell that Jack could weave!

It may be of interest that the music used on the later *Out of Town* programmes came about when one day there was a classical guitarist on Southern's regional magazine programme, *Day by Day*. Jack was walking past the studio and heard the guitarist playing. He immediately fell in love with the piece and later asked the guitarist if he could use it on *Out of Town*.

The *Out of Town* programmes at Southern were originally recorded onto 2 inch video tape. I think later it may have gone onto 1 inch, but certainly when I first was involved 2 inch was the size used. Southern also had a policy of recording the sound of the whole programme on ¼ inch audio tape and just a few of these have survived in storage. Please note though these ¼ inch tapes were left to free run, so they would not sync up with any programme. Also the only visual recording of the studio links were on the 2 inch tape and most of this material has disappeared.

After Southern lost their franchise, I worked with Jack over a period of three years on 60 programmes for Channel 4, called *Old Country* and using the same format and set that had been used at Southern for *Out of Town*. I spent hundreds of hours with Jack as not only was I the producer of the programme and owner of Lacewing Productions (later to become The Production Unit) but I was also the editor of the film inserts.

Old Country was the first full network programme that Jack ever made, so it was a very important stage in Jack's broadcasting career.

As you will know from Jack's story as written by Paul Peacock in this book, Jack did not need a script, it was all in his head, absorbed from the scenes he had seen and anecdotes he had heard over the years, and of course from the doing of country things. When he went out to film he took only one cameraman with him, Stan Bréhaut in Southern Television days and Steve Wagstaff during the *Old Country* days. The cameraman filmed while Jack fished, or watched a saddler, a cart maker, a hurdler, or tacked up his pony and hopped up behind on the flat cart. The filming was done without sound being recorded, and Jack and cameraman worked intuitively together, with minimal need for talk.

As with *Out of Town,* for *Old Country* Jack would sit in the cutting room, look at the rushes and brief me, as editor, on the stories for the programmes. Jack worked with the minimum of fuss and he could do this with people he knew and trusted.

In the case of the *Old Country* series of sixty programmes, when a batch of programmes were ready, Meonstoke Village Hall was hired as the 'studio' and Jack's shed set was erected on the stage, complete with its collection of tools and the missing side wall through which Jack was filmed. Facing Jack would be two cameras and cameramen, the floor manager, lighting crew, sound man with the microphone on a boom, make-up, continuity and others. A small monitor was placed to one side, on which Jack could watch the pictures of the edited stories. In addition there were the director, production assistant and another sound recordist, who at Meonstoke were positioned outside in a broadcast van for the actual recording.

Jack on set in Meonstoke Village Hall, Steve Wagstaff on camera.

The crew and Jack worked intensively, running through the programme first and then filming, just as was done at Southern Television. When everyone was ready, the title sequence for the programme would be run and as the music faded Jack would start spot on cue, talking unscripted straight to camera, an ability that left his audience feeling that he was actually there in their living rooms. As the programme came towards the end, the floor manager would hold up ten fingers and mouth, "Ten, nine, eight, seven, six, five, four, three, two, one," and Jack would round up his story without a stumble, ending on the count of zero with a goodbye and a promise to be back next week.

Jack had an incredible memory and a rare gift as a raconteur. On the occasions when the crew took a late lunch in the local Indian restaurant he would have the whole staff and customers entertained with his stories. As he was generous with his stories, so he was with the tips – the crew were never quite sure if he realised that the note he left on the table was £20 (a lot of money then) instead of the more regular £5 that would have been ten per cent of the bill.

There are Foresters (New Forest folk) who say that Jack's stories were stolen from tales he heard told in the pub, and that he got them wrong. If a few were 'stolen' (well aren't many good stories gleaned from others) Jack certainly gave them the best telling, and if he was ever wrong with his facts he was the first to say that he liked to be told – after all it showed that people were listening and every correction added to his store of knowledge.

Appendix

A selection of writings by Jack and others

When power first came to farming
Yesterday's Country 1992

We have learned to ignore the helicopter and to accept the noise of the silage cutters emerging all around this place that used to be so quiet. Once upon a time, when the wind was right, we could hear the stable clock striking at the manor over beyond the parish boundary. When it was our day for the 'threshing box' we could catch the sound of the steam engine dragging it towards us an hour before it hove in sight.

At one point along the journey the clank of the wheels would stop and the note of the engine change. They had stopped to throw their pipe over the stone bridge by the brook. This was the place for filling up the boiler.

Later the sound would stop altogether for a while. They had reached the lonely Waggoners' Arms. This was the place for filling up the driver.

In its day the threshing machine was a monumental step in mechanisation, putting out of date a thousand flails that had slapped on the threshing floor since Anglo-Saxon times.

It performed the last step of harvest. Everything else had been done by the muscles of horses and people. The corn cut with the binder. The sheaves stacked in the stook to be visited daily by the farmer who would rub out an ear and blow the husk away from the grain to discover whether it had enough 'field-room'. It had to be just ripe enough to travel without shedding, yet dry enough not to moulder in the stack.

It was carried to the rick-yard in the great waggons and the sheaves were delivered to the builders by the elevator, turned by an old horse that walked endlessly in dozy circles.

At night the uncovered stacks were protected by a huge rick-sheet that was hauled up on two posts like the masts of a ship.

Then the stacks were carefully straw thatched, neat and sound, and trimmed at the edges with sheep shears.

However short a time it might be before the first corn was threshed, there was a danger that late thunderstorms could ruin the whole year's production. Readers of Thomas Hardy know all about this from Chapter 36 of 'Far from the Madding Crowd'.

At last the engine trundled onto our place, among the barking of dogs and the scattering of chickens. It ran the box between two of the stacks, which were built just far enough apart to allow two to be worked without shifting the gear. The flywheel of the engine was connected to the machine with a vast, flapping canvas belt that would bring sweat to the brow of a modern safety officer. Then the whistle blew and the bowels of the box began to rattle, and rumble.

Now was the time for the dogs and the boys. A circle of chicken wire was set up on sticks to form a killing ground. The terriers panted with excitement. Each boy brandished the ratting stick that he had chosen from the hedge for its perfect weight and curve.

As the stack was pulled apart and the sheaves tossed into the box, thousands of rats would rush to escape. All day long this juvenile battle went on around the men who were shifting the bags of separated grain and stacking up the separated straw.

I still have the best ratting-stick I ever found. When I was young there were still a few small men who would cut an acre of corn with a scythe and thresh it with a flail. Now I am old there are still a few threshing machines holding out among the combine harvesters. So, I and the threshing box have lived our lives exactly alongside one another.

September Song
The Field 1990

The Frenchman is to the grey what the rainbow is to the brown. There's a cryptic statement! If the meaning is immediately clear to you, then I should enjoy talking with you about the countryside – and I should expect you to sympathise with me about partridges.

Seventy years ago, I used to stand at the yard gate as the dusk fell and listen to the cock partridges calling the coveys together. It was a native English sound, and yet a wild call from the pest. I imagined one evening that it might be the whistle of a wild man from long age with a painted face, hidden behind the hedge of our Big Ground.

Have you ever wondered where the partridge got his name? I never did, until in one of the oldest works, I saw the word spelt 'ptyriche'. I looked at it and it realised they were trying to write down a sound - something like 'putirrachy' – the call of the partridge. I mean the Grey Partridge, the one that belongs here.

The arrival of Prince Albert, which brought us the Christmas tree, was also I fancy responsible for the first sad turn in the story of the Grey Partridge. From the Sehless estates of his Central European relatives there came to England a new kind of shooting. Briefly, the notion was that the ladies and gentlemen should settle themselves in comfort in the park, around which at a great distance had been arranged a ring of peasants. As the circle moved forwards, all the game within were driven to the centre point. There they could be shot to the accompaniment of wine drinking and polite conversation.

A hundred and fifty years ago, old Stonehenge, writing in *The Field* magazine railed against the importation. He called it 'the Continental Battue'. In England it developed into 'Driven Game Shooting'. Stonehenge said that the new way would destroy the dog work – said that was the real pleasure of shooting.

In the centuries before this, the partridge had been perused in England by groups of three or four sportsmen assisted by wonderfully clever dogs. In the earliest times they went with nets which were spread to be pulled over a whole covey hidden in the rough. They had dogs that were trained to crouch low as they pointed in order that the net could be drawn over their backs – 'Setters' in fact.

Later they went with the earliest sporting guns and walked miles in a day. They stalked the partridge on his own ground, conducting a series of tactical manoeuvres in terms of the wind and weather, the lie of the ground and the state of the season. Every outing involved a different set of chess moves; and everyone on the shoot had to understand exactly what he was doing. Their muzzle loading guns allowed for only intermittent shooting and caused them to proceed hung about with powder flasks, shot belts, ramrods, cap boxes and pockets full of wade that had been stamped out of discarded beaver hats. But they were men of patience and moderation. They didn't expect to fill their bags. Four and a half brace would send a man home triumphant.

It was an art and it all depended on the wonderful dogs, from the best strains of Spanish pointer, brought back by Wellington's officers from the Peninsular, to some very clever creatures of much less distinction.

My father was a Field Spaniel man, but his dogs could lift a foreleg and shove out their noses with the best. With them we were taught to walk the wild coveys on our farmland. "Honour the dog," he used to say. "If she hadn't a better nose than you have, we wouldn't be buying her rations."

By the time 'driven game' took over, the rich were into breech-loading guns, with cartridges that gave immediate reloading. A man could stand square in one place, in line with others of consequence, and have game flown over his head in a continuing serial salute. Stonehenge was right. They didn't need the dogs or, at least, only dogs to fetch and carry. "Servants' Hall Dogs" is what my father called Retrievers. "Ought to be wearing a damned apron." We had entered the age of the pheasant.

The Grey Partridge was unsuited to Victorian self-aggrandisement. It was difficult to present in one place in large numbers. It was difficult to breed domestically, and birds so bred were distressed and flustered when put in the 'silkie broodies', or incubators, into open country. If penned in numbers, they struggled to escape and disperse widely in search of territories.

The attempts continued. There was some purist resistance. For a long while the Field Certificate, issued as a mark of excellence to Game Farms, required an undertaking not to deal in English partridge eggs. So birds were imported from Hungary or Czechoslovakia.

In the end they turned to the Red-legged Partridge that Charles II had tried without success to establish at Windsor after his return from the Continent. The red-legged Frenchman is a dapper yuppy with the heart of a pheasant. He will venture into woods. He runs a long way before rising. When he does fly, he flies straight, without the challenging aerobatics of the native bird.

But his different call has now replaced the 'putirrachy' of the old Grey cocks. He is now the common species in England, alongside the strew-bred Rainbows that are poured annually into the streams where we used to fish for the wild Brown Trout.

Lord Russell - who was, after all, a Socialist - said that you can ruin almost anything by trying to make it available to everybody.

Modern farming has sprayed away the weed seeds on which the Grey loved to feed, and the insects needed by its chicks. It has substituted early silage for hay crops, eliminated the majority of the stubbles and shaved those remaining close with the combine.

Yet man believes he can master all problems of nature. Not so long ago, a millionaire of modern agriculture set out to show that the partridge could be bent to man's will. He announced he would break the record for a partridge day. With months of preparation and masses of money and an army of helpers he made preparations. Finally, on the appointed day and in the presence of press cameras, he succeeded. Twelve hundred brace, was it? I prefer not to try to remember.

Very few people have the resources for such an enterprise and recently a friend of mine was told by a friend of his that partridge were no more than a nuisance. It was impossible to get together enough for ten guns. "Then why," my friend replied, "Don't you try with two guns and some dogs?" Indeed! But where would you find the terrain on which the old way could be applied?

Perhaps when some of the modern well-to-do, whose average age is now so much younger, relax sufficiently in their prosperity to cease displaying it and seek again for cultivated ways of doing things, and when the intensity of farming fades and parts of the old landscape we affect to be preserving have a chance to reappear; perhaps then the voice of the old Grey cocks will be heard in the land.

We have, after all, a wider choice of good pointing breeds that have been imported by the rough shooters, who have carried on in the meanwhile. They could be selectively bred and trained for a retrieval of the old way. Not least, since I was recently concerned with the training of the first few to come to England, the admirable Brittany Pointing Spaniels.

Getting Keepers Taped
The Field

In 1945, a British Army Field Broadcasting Unit, under Captain John McMillan of the South Wales Borderers, later to be Managing Director of Rediffusion Television, discovered next to Lord Haw-Haw's bunker in the basement of Hamburg Radio three large machines, each in a steel case marked 'Magnetophpon' and weighing at least a hundredweight.

Two were reported to Signals, at the time too busy to think about them, but with a Service cunning born of five years of war to which no modern street-wisdom could hold a candle, it was decided to smuggle the other one back to the BBC in exchange for some OBA8 amplifiers the unit badly needed.

It was a chancy operation. It even involved bullying the ENSA officer into providing an alto saxophone for the Naval jazz group then forming in Hamburg. But it succeeded and seventy-two hours later the Corporation's engineers were the first men of the free world to examine the workings of a tape recorder.

That moment stirred again in my memory when I looked over the two brace of books on gamekeeping which I bagged this week.

We used not to have books by gamekeepers. Scratching out a list of birds in a notebook was about as far as they went. They could communicate their knowledge, as any apprenticed lad would witness, but not in a written way.
So we heard about them second-hand. Country gentlemen with pen names spoke of them rather loftily. We treasure the words of 'Bickerdyke' who said that when winter fishing you should take the man along so that in case of frost he could be told to suck the ice from your rod rings.

Working writers who had chosen the country scene wrote about them, but created a picture suited to the readers' fantasies rather than reality. Richard Jefferies, who started it all with 'The Gamekeeper at Home', was far from innocent of that.

But now the gamekeeper, along with the aircraft controller, the pop artist, the interviewed criminal and the stockbroker, speaks freely into the perfected descendants of the Magnetophon. The editor then shapes it all up and it is the editor that matters.

The best of my four current books was spoken by Evan Rogers.

> By the time you have finished you will know this wonderful 82-year-old as if you had lived alongside him; his immersion in one patch of the countryside for 62 years on end, his unbookish knowledge of every living thing in it, his grinding industry, his chauvinism, the hardness that came from dealing in life and death and dangerous poachers, his sympathy for rogues, his understanding of his masters, with love for some and contempt for others.

> In keeping with the media fashion for hearing from the people without adulteration the editor, Clive Murphy, has done as little as possible. Perhaps too little. Five pages on end without paragraphing are very hard work. It is, after all, being made into a text and sometimes spelling is surrendered to phonetics. It takes a moment to realise that 'off omwud' is 'off homeward'. But I niggle. The job is above criticism.

The editor of the book recorded by John Foyster (he is Keith Proud, well-known on Cleveland Radio) has a more spooky presence.

> The ghost seems to have slipped in his two-cents-worth. Despite the alibi of the keeper's devotion to Southwold library, the bits of mediaeval history, the Norman-French derivation of the word to poach, and other such, have for me a smack of the broadcast researcher. And as for the statement that moleskins were chiefly used for making labourer's trousers, I'll bet that didn't come from the keeper! I have long ago seen a waistcoat of them, but moleskin trousers were always made, as they are now, from the Lancashire cotton cloth that bears that nickname. To any man who can convince me he has seen a pair of working pants sewn up from hundreds of little grey pelts I will donate five gallons of good cider.

> But it is an excellent book and contains the best yet description of gamekeeper's techniques of breeding, rearing, presentation and shoot organisation, all told by John Foyster as an account of how

he was taught them in stages during his learning years.

In sad contrast, with the two books from Nimrod Press, we are back in Grub Street.

> This is the scribbler working his patch. The information is second-hand and either trivial or hopelessly padded. The structure is disorganised. The illustrations are either incompetent modern sketches or inappropriate out of copyright pictures badly reproduced.

For the differences between the new-style and the old-style books on gamekeeping we must offer a small vote of thanks to Captain McMillan and his gallant lads.

Know How - an information programme for children

This is the original memo that led to the iconic TV show, *HOW?*
20 February 1964

This proposal is for a thirty minute studio-originated information programme for children, intended for transmission every week at 5.25 p.m. - perhaps on Thursday - and follows the Programme Board's recent approval of such an idea in principle.

KNOW HOW is based on the assumption that children are interested in 'knowledge' if it is presented with a sense of fun, and if they can participate in it.

In KNOW HOW every item is based directly on a child's written request for the item and every child is is directly involved in his or her item, wether it is in the studio or on film.

KNOW HOW, like the feature page of a newspaper, will consist of both fully developed items and quick 'spot' items. The programme will have a permanent linkman, and three or four specialists. I would like to have Jack Hargreaves introduce the programme (for an initial 13-week period), act as editorial adviser, and to be involved in relevant items.

KNOW HOW - some sample elements:

'How do they...?' A contemporary series including 'How do they catch smugglers?' made with the Customs. 'How do they put fires out? made with the Fire Brigade. 'How do they bring a big ship up to Southampton?' made with the Harbour Pilot. 'How do they make a young actor look like an old man?' made with the Make-Up Department, etc.

How do animals...? This item, from the London Zoo, is given a 'how' point in order that children can understand the adaptions that make animals what they are. 'How do animals get their food?' - giraffes have long necks so they can graze off trees, so we will the giraffe some carrots on the end of a twenty-five foot pole. We will give the anteater some honey and ants eggs down the other end of a vacuum cleaner extension tube - with his long nose and his tongue he'll be able to reach them. 'How do animals get along?' with kangaroo hopping, the snake crawling, the seahorse, the caterpillar, the agile gibbons swinging from branch to branch.

'How does it feel to...?' In this spot we let the children themselves realise ambitions and daydreams; the 'I've always wanted to' element of every child's imagination. 'How does it feel to be weightless? 'How does it feel to be rescued by helicopter? 'How does it feel to climb a mountain?' 'How does it feel to ride in a tank?' 'How does it feel to walk in a mannequin parade?' 'How does it feel to jump on a champion pony?'

The above examples serve to show not only the scope for 'information' elements, but also the fundamental idea on which KNOW HOW is built that learning is fun. Within this format we can deal with a great range of subjects - science, sport, natural history, hobbies, adventures, etc.

Cyril Bennet, John Rhodes and Jack Hargreaves

A letter to the *Daily Mail*

When Virginia Ironside gave Jack a 'going over' in the *Daily Mail*, a lot of people wrote in to complain. Isobel was one of them:

Dear Sir,

I thought the job of a TV critic was to criticise TV programmes. Virginia Ironside seems to prefer to destroy the character and integrity of the people who make them – an economical method, by which a whole series can be written off at a stroke, without the bother of even seeing the programmes.

Her attack on Jack Hargreaves was so startlingly full of inaccuracies that it would be pointless to start listing them. However, in the entire piece I did find one true fact, for which I am happy to vouch. Yes, his neckerchief is pressed. I know because I do it. (Surprise, surprise, Miss Ironside, people in the country not only wash, but actually iron too!)

I can only think that poor little Miss Ironside is so deeply embedded in the bidet-duvet-fondue world of the mass media that she no longer knows the real thing when she sees it and has to try to prove that people like Jack are phonies too. Not a chance, Miss Ironside. Why don't you creep out from under that typewriter and come down here and face a few facts. And bring your gumboots.

The Days of the Drowners *Yesterday's Country* June 1990

In the two telephone books that cover most of the old Kingdom of Wessex you will find the people whose name is Mead or Meader or Meaden. This is no accident. These were the people who looked after the water meadows.

It was here in our countryside, where the great chalk mass gathered the year's rain and delivered it pure and cool from ten thousand springs, that the water meadows flourished. Like many country things that people would like to keep for ever, they were a temporary phase of agriculture. The Cavaliers and Roundheads knew them not. The Second World War farmers, driving their lease-lend tractors, watched them die.

Up until later Jacobean times the rivers that carried off the chalk water - the Test, Itchen, Kennett, Meon Allen and Avon - were flanked on each side by marshes that ran from the water's edge out to where the land began to rise.
In this dense, damp wilderness the Water Rails crept, the bitterns boomed and the fisherman's bunting whistled. Yellow-Flags, Bog Bean, Frogbit and Pink Balsam grew in open patches. Forests of thatching reed stood six foot high.

The idea of the water-meadows was simple, but the task of building them intimidating. First a big ditch had to encircle the marsh, curving round to rejoin the river lower down at a big sluice gate. Along this the water could be drained off the marsh. It was known as the 'draught' or sometimes the 'gutter'. There is still a farm track close to me, with a big ditch along it, that is known as Gutter Lane.

Then you dug 'carriers' in herring-bone fashion, from river to draught, each again with its own sluice gate.

It took a century and a half to build this system through the Wessex valleys. It was all done by men with spades. The country people must have talked about it incessantly. Advisory engineers were everywhere, contracted to the landlords. Labour was brought in from the Low Countries. Deals were done with the millers for the supply of water. Some even closed their water mills and made a living by rationing water to the mead owners below at so many hours a day. Fierce legal actions were fought when one man's engineering worked to the disadvantage of his neighbours.

In every village the Meaders became established. They were locally known as the Drowners. In March the meads were flooded and an early spring 'bite' was fed to the sheep who came in for rationed meal times as 'couples', ewe and lamb together. In early summer a lush crop of hay was cut with scythes and then the 'aftermath' grazed by bullocks. Winter was spent cleaning the carriers and mending sluices.

I saw it all die, the system that founded the Wessex corn and sheep economy. Tractors couldn't move in to work the water-bound strips. Silage took the place of hay. Concentrated feeds made early feeding easy. I came on leave to find Italian prisoners dredging the rivers to get the water off the meads for the growing of much needed wartime corn.

Afterwards there were still a few old men about who were proud to be called 'Drowner'. One of them told me how, in the late spring, the best scythe-men were carted in wagons to Reading to be picked up by Royal waggonette and taken to mow the old Queen's grass.

He spoke of the great beef dinners that were served to them and of the Royal barn in which they slept in the straw. On his wall was a faded photograph, taken in front of Windsor Castle, of the fifty men who were spoken of as the Queen's Drowners.

Out of Town and *Old Country* broadcasts

Between first transmission in 1960 to final programme at the end of 1981, over one thousand *Out of Town* films were transmitted. At peak it attracted audiences of one and a quarter million and was considered a vanguard in outside broadcasting. Here, published for the first time, is the full listing of all the programmes of which only some twenty eight remain intact.

July 1960
Pack horse
Fly catching
Clay pigeon
Horse drawn vehicles

August 1960
Prep. Pigeon shoot
Dog training
Electric fishing
Sea fishing

September 1960
Pigeon shooting
Pony scramble
Crayfish fishing
Tench fishing
Pistol shooting

October 1960
Chinchilla breeding
Pheasant shooting
Pike fishing
Country objects

November 1960
Pike fishing
Dog training
Sea angling
Fishing in flood

December 1960
Badgers
DIY objects
Police dogs
Sea angling

January 1961
Catamaran sailing
Pike fishing
Winter work
Angling Championships

February 1961
Fibreglass boats
Ground bait
Portrait of a canal
Go-Kart racing
Roach spinning

March 1961
Preserved bait
Beagle hunt
Fishing from a boat
Hare shoot

April 1961
Fly fishing
Ferret hunting
Cross Channel trip

May 1961
Chinese junk
A country walk
Trailing boats
Salmon fishing

June 1961
Racing pigeons
Mayfly
Tope fishing
Cannes trip

July 1961
Arrival of lifeboat
Work at Lymington
Pony racing
Sand lining

August 1961
Camping ridgeway
Chub fishing
Solent yachting
Pigeon shooting

September 1961
Conversion of lifeboat
Sea Scouts
Baseball
Owls
Perch fishing

October 1961
Duck shooting
Inshore trawling
Gliding
Pier Angling Festival

November 1961
Fishing from a boat
Nest box making
Pike fishing
Designing a yacht

December 1961
Water trials of yacht
Maps
High Spots - clips
Red Shank
Flounder fishing

January 1962
Boxing Day
Repair of damaged boat
Country objects
Care of guns

February 1962
Boat Show
Pigeon shooting
Pony racing
Pike fishing

March 1962
Building DANICA
New Forest pony deaths
Boat fishing
Work on boat
Mending hole in boat

April 1962
Pigeon decoys
Lymington harbour
Firing a musket
Skate fishing

May 1962
Salmon fishing
Repairing boat
Rabbiting
DANICA crossing Channel

June 1962
Cow Pony riding
Unusual dog breeds
Lake trout
Sand eels
Bass fishing

July 1962
Gulls eggs
Perch fishing
Christiana
Chub fishing

August 1962
Tope fishing
Mackerel fishing
Shooting people
Gymkhana
Mullet fishing

September 1962
Bloodhounds
Pigeon shooting
Angler's other eye
Dinghy race

October 1962
Stour Angling Competition
Rowing regatta
Horse training

November 1962
Bait casting
Dog fishing
Donkey derby
Going to work by boat
Fishing gadgets

December 1962
Hats
Scrapbook
Seine netting
Shooting

January 1963
Scrapbook
Fly fishing
Winter countryside
Club boats

February 1963
Decoy setting
Thames roach fishing
Benson lock
Weymouth fishing

March 1963
Norse people
Thames angling
Fly tying
Deer shoot
Long line fishing

May 1963
Michael Law - sailing
Lifeboat conversion and landing

June 1963
Season's first tope
Mackerel fishing
Crossbows

July 1963
School pony trek
Lobster potting
Fishing for eighteen pence

August 1963
Turbot fishing
Single handed sailing
Tench and trout fishing

September 1963
Sea trout
Sea trials of Blackbird
Pike fishing
Pheasant shooting

October 1963
Pony driving
Run about boats
Pigeon shooting
Dace fishing

November 1963
Night fishing
Brown Bess
Grayling

December 1963
Ponies
Pheasant shoot
Ferreting

January 1964
Beach Boys
Pony races
Sprats
Shooting lesson
Flounders

173

February 1964
Speed at sea
Roach on Avon
Traffic jam afloat

March 1964
Fishing authors

April 1964
Eel spearing
Dinghies
Pointers

May 1964
Gulls eggs
Gwynneth
Small trout
Electric fishing
Hamble scramble

June 1964
Mayfly
Fancy dress
Bass from shore

July 1964
Bass from boats
Irish journey
Irish fishing
Traction engines

August 1964
Paolo steering gear
Show jumping pictures

September 1964
Fibreglass boats
Coarse fishing
Grayling
Pony and cart race

October 1964
Perch fishing
German pointers
Flounders
Dosh netting
Tuck netting

November 1964
Pond fishing
Eel fishing
Phyllia outboard
Dover congar

December 1964
Grayling
Pigeon shooting
Fishing books
Christmas spirit

January 1965
River pollution
Bournemouth beach
Beagles
Clay pigeons
Churchill tribute

February 1965
Boat show
Wild duck
Fresh water mussels
Colonel Walker

March 1965
Flounders
Stock fish
Coarse fishing
Pigeons

April 1965
Beam trawl
Muzzle loader
Beach fishing
Dog training
Sea sickness

May 1965
Whippets
Trout fishing
Fishing tackle exhibition
Skate

June 1965
Boat on wheels
Two lakes
Bream & Casting

July 1965
Coarse fishing
Co-op boats
Lobsters
Chub
Bird marking

August 1965
Brook trout
Otter hounds
Sea sleds
Pony driving

September 1965
Electric fishing
Perch fishing
Solent boats
Learning to fish

October 1965
Trot line
Shanklin club
Jorrocks
Minnow bottle
French canal

November 1965
DIY boat
Perch
Mink and crayfish
Dog work

December 1965
Roach
Ferrets
Christmas books
Canterbury pike
Cod fishing

January 1966
Gun handling
Pike from punt
Young Tiger
Picking up

February 1966
In town
Thatching
Lobster pots

March 1966
Punt
Last fish of the season
Dog training
New Forest beagles

April 1966
Two lakes first fish
Bess - Dog training

May 1966
National Angler's Council
Introduction to Deal
Tackle show
New Forest ride

June 1966
Six weeks of French films on the Camargue

July 1966
Carp
Langstone

August 1966
Fly casting
Kinsale competition
Fibreglass punt
Barbel

September 1966
Fishing competition
Bluebell
Rabbits and dogs

October 1966
Sea fishing finals
Casting demonstration
Bess
Varne

November 1966
Arnold Wiles
Plaice
Pike fishing
Boy in a boat

December 1966
Lymington ferry
Three weeks about Cyprus
New Forest pony races

January 1967
Cod fishing
Boat show
Kennel
Punt

February 1967
Underwater
No pike

March 1967
Electric fishing
Vets
Jobs in the farm
Branding cattle farewell

July 1967
Elsdale boat/Dace
Black bream
Musical ride
Cockles

August 1967
Deal heat
Pony trekking
Langstone heat
Horse dale

September 1967
Pigeon shooting
Pony trek
Gale
Gymkhana
Garden fish

October 1967
Kinsale
Freshwater championship
Carriages
Tackle

November 1967
Donkey and pike
Perch
Pony sale
Flounder and eel

December 1967
Ploughing match
Cod fishing
Christmas presents
Foot and mouth fishing
Review of the year

January 1968
Owen and Donket
Winter and summer
Rough shooting
Pike fishing

February 1968
Sprats
Pigeon flighting
Charter boats
Riversdale

March 1968
Spigot rods
Owen
Reel and roach
Old ponies and Italian ponies
Drascombe lugger

June 1968
Tribute to Ollie and puppies
Nesting boxes and spotted horse

175

July 1968
Easi worm
Orphan foal
Romney marsh
Horses eyes & eyesight

August 1968
Stingray
The little river

September 1968
Plaice and thrifty
Pigeons and puppies
Carp
Donkey cart

October 1968
Shell fish (Normandy)
Stallions (Normandy)
Bass and heats
Donkey and October

November 1968
Kinsale final
French dogs (Normandy)
Country fair (Normandy)
Sam
Frome fishing

December 1968
Clay pigeons and Ollie
Christmas presents
deal cod
400 programmes

January 1969
R.S.P.C.A. (Ringwood)
Christmas events
Skipper's holiday
Freshwater competition
Flatties (Flounder competition at IOW)

February 1969
Pike fishing
Roach fishing
Pigeon shooting
Bess and Ollie
Winter grass (Mr Jackman)

March 1969
Orkney 1
Bournemouth boat show - Parade
Billy Lane/George Feesey match
Orkney 2

April 1969
Finale

September 1969
Heats of championship
Bulls and stallions

October 1969
Orkney final
Bog roach
Duck fighting
Fly fishing for dace
The pony ride (Gracie)

November 1969
The pike pool
Steam engines
Bass fishing
Trotting trials

December 1969
Lobsters
Mares and foals
Grayling
Biggleswade

January 1970
Pheasant shoot
Cod fishing
Pigeon shooting
Roach fishing (flooded water)
Greenhouse

February 1970
Gardening
Boat roach fishing
Donkey cart
Romney marsh frozen lake

March 1970
Driving Sam and horse sales
Pilot Jack and Dormouse
Close season trout
Trout - Two lakes

April 1970
Western riding
Gardening
Rare bushy tailed dormouse
Burley show
Fly fishing - River Allen

May 1970
Roe deer
Enton Lake fisheries
Plaice fishing

October 1970
Heats of sea angling championship
Final of championship in Orkney
Pigeon shooting
Tench fishing

November 1970
Trotting trials
Black bream
Chislet
Rabbiting

December 1970
Seashore
Taxi drivers
Christmas presents
Cod

January 1971
Clay pigeons
Ponies and trout
River Avon
Pheasant shooting
Fast water

February 1971
*Codling and duck
Shooting
Frost
Cottage*

March 1971
*Pony cart
Bournemouth boat show
Cold morning
End of season*

September 1971
*Two lake fly fishing
Flowers and birds*

October 1971
*Colonel Hawker
Black bream
Rudd family
Roach - Frank Guttfield*

November 1971
*Zoo fishing
Squirrels and garden
Trotting trial
Prawns and Q.17*

December 1971
*Spaniels
Lake fishing
Pups and 14ft dinghy
Crustaceans
Cod with Ron Edwards
and son*

January 1972
*Calendar
Drug fishing
Duck shooting
Dace and no perch*

February 1972
*Wheelwright
Grayling
Q.23
Roach in a factory*

March 1972
*Storm (the pony) and wild
horses
Pike
Pigeon shooting
Ringwood market
Perch fishing - Sid
Toovey*

April 1972
*Hacksaw
Flu
Preview of boat show
Spring*

May 1972
*Souvenirs
Cottages
Fly fishing - River Test
Shetland - birds*

June 1972
*Shetland - trout
Ponies
Shetland - skate
Orchids
Chub and trout*

September 1972
*Vine at New cottage
Roach/Rudd
Shetland final*

October 1972
*Testing Tom
Tench
Fungus and cod at
Broadstairs
Two lakes and migratory
birds*

November 1972
*Guildford market and
currant bun fungus
Drovers dogs and
lurchers
Low water and making a
lake
Marsh birds and
Workmate*

December 1972
Rough shoot and Daisy

June 1973
*Stage coach and rabbits
Hebrides - Sea fishing
and new born calf
Trout and seaweed and
wagtails*

July 1973
*Phil Coles and boys
fishing
Working horses and J.H.
& Horse and cart
Exploding bait box and
Young Farmers rally
Kentish pond and lobster
moult*

August 1973
*Casting champions
Southall market and Kent
duck shoot
Herne Bay bass and
insects
Golden Horseshoe ride
Secret Brook*

September 1973
*History walk and farm
animals
Sea angling final
Mayfly
Lochs and birds*

October 1973
*Cod fishing and cobs
Appleby
Mackerel fishing
Axe men pub sales
Autumn scene
Startops*

November 1973
*Birds and nest boxes
River Nadder and electric
fishing
Spaniels and cattle drift
Beagles
Peter Deane - Fly tying*

177

December 1973
*Christmas presents 2/Spain
Journey downstream/Red spinners
Spain 2
Horses and bullfights*

January 1974
*Pheasant shoot and fish marketing
Promise of summer
Spanish mules & Yerro mule
Martins lake*

February 1974
*Dog's tail and caravans
Hacienda 1
Seasons in the Farden
Wind and weather*

March 1974
*Hacienda 2
Broommaker and saddler
Woods and ferrets
Answer to correspondence/Yerro*

October 1974
*Hebrides finals/Game fair/Parade of dogs
Young things
Race-maker/high school horse
Trammel netting/wheelwright*

November 1974
*Fishing - Itchen New Water
Learning to shoot
Kent lakes
Mower/round up
Peeler crabs/knappeting*

December 1974
*Forest carts/Dinghy
Christmas presents
Grayling/Lining carts
Rhododendrons*

January 1975
*Jack's calendar
Partridges/Daisy's day
Borman's Pond/STV S.A.C.
Yerro's operation
River Meon/Stallions*

February 1975
*Echo Sounder/Farm sale
Field trial. Mudcat.
Caravan/Water works*

March 1975
*Fishing floats/Puppy training
Growing shets/Poole boat show
Pea sharks/Donkey cart wheels
Favourite things*

January 1976
*Poacher/Country sports fair 1
Protected marsh/Country sports fair 2
Old farm implements
Carbon fibre rod/Picking up
Boxing Day races/Studio items*

February 1976
*Butterflies/North wind
Burley horse show/Dressage
South wind
G.S. Pointers
Secret brook*

March 1976
*Southall market/Kent Duck
(Bygone studio props)
Sawing
Heavy horses/Gypsy wedding
Review of season's films*

September 1976
*Lilies in gravel pits/Charcoal burners
Goat/Hawthorn
Corn harvest/Big tench
Forest fire/Pole fishing*

October 1976
*Day at the races/Bantam 1 & 2
Tailing/Oak, deer, acorns
Road to the Isles/Leaping fish 1
Rabbit show/Leaping fish 2/Perch/Gravel pits
Brickworks*

November 1976
*Smithy/Fishing in a gale
Saddle maker
Tug of War/Dace and duck
Mole catcher/Ringwood market*

December 1976
*Hurdle maker/Sheep fair
Deer shoot
Xmas special 1
Xmas special 2*

February 1977
Spring perch

March 1977
*Ferrets/Calf market
Bygones/Blacksmith
Young and sons/Dahlias
Roach/Pub games*

April 1977
*Fox hounds/Marlborough horse fair
Cape carts/Brook trout
Hedging/Pike fishing
Trout/Heavy horses
British finches*

December 1978
Xmas presents
Spring walk/Pushpenny
Stow fair/Tomatoes
Mayfly/Garden tools

January 1979
Opening day/Shoot sale
Rabbits/Mr Quinton
Lake roach/Circus
Mass of bloom/Wreck fishing

February 1979
Lobsters/Poultry show
Bar skittles/Legering
Ferrets/Tractor pull
Onion stringing
Donkeys/Dace fishing

March 1979
Tug of War/Turkey lake
Cider making
Chalk

April 1979
Lake/Shorthorns/Freesians
Winter Stour/Sunshine in Qatar
Fishing in the Gulf

May 1979
Arab garden
Use of training horses in Qatar

June 1979
Heavy horses
Highland cattle in Hampshire/The Oryx
Habitat/Oryx hunt

October 1980
Flowering trees/Fishing final - Islay
Judging gardens/Kennett trout
Cart models/Learning to cast
Fell ponies/San Foin
Heavy horses/Canal tench

November 1980
Braiding horses/Whitewater mayfly
Circus painting/Pollack
Sheep dipping/Bite indicator
Appleby show/Greg lake

December 1980
Barbel/Fred's ferrets
Pigeon shooting/Dog nobblers
Christmas presents

January 1981
Freeze branding/Perch Calendar
Pigs/River Test
Strawberry cart/Grayling
Sheepdog sale/Gun collection

February 1981
Bassets/Beach casting
Threshing/Fell fishing
Lurchers/Hambledon Hill
Pheasants/Trade carts
Dogs, clocks and onions

Old Country – transmitted once a week by Channel 4

January 1983
*Walking sticks/Hurdlemaker
Mayfly trout/Todber Stone
Stow fair/Flat cart
Garden/Cut Mill*

February 1983
*Harnessing a horse/
Decent dog
Sheepfair/Dabchick
Fishing rods/Morey's Lake*

March 1983
*Tarrant Valley/Circus
Lurchers/Rabbiting
Cutting up a pig
Downland/Cattle breeds
Trolly drive/Fiddleford Mill*

April 1983
Pony drift/Goats

May 1983
Brittany spaniels

June 1983
*Bygones
Bygones/Driving*

July 1983
Steam plough/Terrier show

August 1983
*Pigeon shooting/Sturminster Mill
Thatching reed/Hound show
Pack pony/Turk's pond*

April 1984
*Harvest/Flapping
Blagdon horse/Bass
Grayling/Cartbuilding/Blacksmith
Cart painter/Butterflies*

May 1984
*Children's competition
Cockles/Garden
Foundry/Mackerel/Looksee:
Folly Towers Piddle/Collar maker
Buttons/Turnout*

June 1984
*King's Highway
Steam saw/Tench
Barrelmaker/Onion strings*

July 1984
*Birds and mink/Pacing
Larner tree/Two lakes
Rabbits/Sea float
Deserted village*

August 1984
*Cape cart
Plaice
Appleby/Woolfe's climb*

June 1985
*Skittles
Sheep dipping/
Battlesden carts
Flower drive/Sheep washing
Bantams/Manes and tails*

July 1985
*Spinning/Fjord pony
Driving event
Gudgeon fishing/Lessay dogs
French National Stud/Lessay Fair*

August 1985
*Potter/Artificial insemination
Huntaway dog/Pole fishing
Boadicea's Horses/Duncliffe Hill*

September 1985
*Horses and cobs/
Chub fishing
Dipper
Long net/Farm sale
Vet's exam/Wickham's fancy*

October 1985
*Cider/Cow's feet
Ponds/River Care
Geese/Mink hunting
Pub crawl*

180